Health Policy Developments 7/8

Reinhard Busse, Sophia Schlette (eds.)

Health Policy Developments 7/8

Focus on Prevention,
Health and Aging,
New Health Professions

| Verlag Bertelsmann**Stiftung**

Bibliographic information published by Die Deutsche Nationalbibliothek

Die Deutsche Nationalbibliothek lists this publication in the
Deutsche Nationalbibliografie; detailed bibliographic information
is available online at http://dnb.d-nb.de

© 2007 Verlag Bertelsmann Stiftung, Gütersloh
Responsible: Sophia Schlette
Copy editor: Celia Bohannon; Precision Editorial Services, Valkenburg, NL
Production editor: Sabine Reimann
Cover design: Nadine Humann
Cover illustration: Aperto AG, Berlin
Typesetting and print: Hans Kock Buch- und Offsetdruck GmbH, Bielefeld
ISBN 978-3-89204-962-3

www.bertelsmann-stiftung.org/publications

Contents

5

Preface

Dear readers,

This version of *Health Policy Developments* has grown considerably in size. We have opted to assemble a double edition large enough to feature the many health-policy laboratories and reform efforts across the 20 countries represented in the International Network Health Policy and Reform. Countries obviously are facing the same challenges of longevity, lifestyle, and chronic conditions—all of which are the achievements of wealth, high levels of education, and progress in medicine and health care. What may be less obvious is that the responses that policy makers are choosing to tackle the commonest challenges are also slowly but surely converging. This remark may come as a surprise. For some time many of us thought that, given the diversity of healthcare systems and of delivery patterns ("path dependency"), and given the very diverse mechanisms of decision-making and of balancing out the interests of many powerful health-policy stakeholders, comparisons would be of limited value. Some said that looking across one's own healthcare system, while no doubt enlightening and nice to do, would largely be a matter of learning about and not of learning from. But in recent years, we have been hearing and reading quite a bit about the convergence or alignment of healthcare systems ("hybrid systems"). And regarding healthcare practice, globalization and technology have brought about mobile patients, flying doctors, traveling x-rays, and—sadly—pandemics that don't stop short of borders or airplanes.

Where does all this take us? Looking into healthcare systems across one's borders is no longer an academic luxury of those of us who are curious enough and do not mind traveling. Learning about and from others to advance and enrich reform options has become part of our work; it has become a necessity for those of us engaged in policy analysis, policy advice, and policy making. Global challenges require strategic responses that will then be implemented in accordance with national or local systems. Here is another recent observation. "New" old principles (equity and solidarity) are again moving up the political agenda—perhaps in response to the limitations of over a decade of market-oriented, individualistic approaches in health and social policies. We see that the social dimension of health- and social-care returns is closely related to quality, choice, and patient participation. It also comes well-tuned with the individual's responsibility in the management of his or her condition, and it comes embedded with tools that help increase efficiency of care.

The cut-across topics of this double edition are
- need-based care and good access
- universal coverage
- patient orientation, shared decision-making and patient choice
- healthful aging, care at home, long-term care
- human resources developments
- drug policy and price setting
- health promotion and prevention

Chapter 1, From Idea to Implementation, for the first time follows the evolution of health-policy ideas in selected countries over a longer period of time.

It analyzes major structural reform processes in the Netherlands, Austria, Great Britain (England), and Finland—from inception to result. Comparing these processes, we can detect the tendency mentioned above toward system convergence, a tendency to align tax-funded and contribution-funded healthcare systems. For instance, in social health insurance systems we observe that the role of the state as the norm-setting and regulatory authority has been strengthened. Examples of this are the introduction of country-wide hospital plans in Austria and the abolishment of the traditional, corporatist self-governance of sickness funds and other actors in the Netherlands. From the other end, the state-funded English NHS is introducing regulatory tools borrowed from the free market. Patients have more choice and voice

in the system, and private providers of healthcare services are encouraged to play. Overall we observe a trend toward the devolution of planning and financial responsibility to lower-level authorities. This way health- and social-care services are expected to better respond to the local population's needs and expectations. To this end, all Austrian regions (*Bundesländer*) are establishing health platforms. Among other responsibilities, the regional platforms can allocate an increasing amount of financial resources to foster integrated delivery systems. In England, Primary Care Trusts (PCTs) hold funds to coordinate and commission both primary and secondary care. In Finland we find a reverse trend that fits into this broader picture just as well: In order to increase efficiency and improve coordination of a variety of community services formerly provided at the level of municipalities, health care, social care and long-term care responsibilities are now bundled in larger geographic units.

Should you be interested in learning more about or from a certain country or reform approach, we will be happy to provide you with additional material or put you in touch with the experts. We hope that this edition provides you with new and useful global insights and local outlooks.

Introduction

The International Network for Health Policy and Reform

Since 2002 the International Network for Health Policy and Reform has brought together health-policy experts from 20 countries around the world to report on current health-reform issues and health-policy developments in their respective countries. Geared toward implementation, the network aims to narrow the gap between research and policy, providing timely information on what works and what does not in health-policy reform.

Participating countries were chosen from a German perspective. We looked for countries with reform experience relevant to Germany. Partner institutions were selected taking into account their expertise in health policy and management, health economics or public health. Our network is interdisciplinary; our experts are economists, political scientists, physicians and lawyers. Many of them have considerable experience as policy advisers. Others are experts in international comparative research.

Table 1: Partner institutions

Australia	Centre for Health Economics, Research and Evaluation (CHERE), University of Technology Sydney
Austria	Institute for Advanced Studies (IHS), Vienna
Canada	Canadian Policy Research Networks (CPRN), Ottawa
Denmark	Institute of Public Health, Health Economics, University of Southern Denmark, Odense
Estonia	PRAXIS, Center for Policy Studies, Tallinn
Finland	STAKES, National Research and Development Center for Welfare and Health, Helsinki
France	IRDES, Institut de Recherche et de Documentation en Economie de la Santé, Paris
Germany	Bertelsmann Stiftung, Gütersloh; Department of Health Care Management, Berlin University of Technology (TUB)
Israel	The Myers-JDC-Brookdale Institute, Smokler Center for Health Policy Research, Jerusalem
Japan	Public Policy School (HOPS), Hokkaido University, Sapporo
The Netherlands	Department of Health Organization, Policy and Economics (BEOZ), Faculty of Health Sciences, University of Maastricht
New Zealand	Centre for Health Services Research and Policy, University of Auckland
Poland	Institute of Public Health, Jagiellonian University, Krakow
Singapore	Department of Community, Occupational and Family Medicine, National University of Singapore (NUS)
Slovenia	Institute of Public Health of the Republic of Slovenia, Ljubljana
South Korea	School of Public Health, Seoul National University
Spain	Research Centre for Economy and Health (Centre de Recerca en Economia i Salut, CRES), University Pompeu Fabra, Barcelona
Switzerland	Institute of Microeconomics and Public Finance (MecoP), Università della Svizzera Italiana, Lugano
United Kingdom	LSE Health & Social Care, London School of Economics and Political Science (LSE)
United States	The Commonwealth Fund, New York; Institute for Global Health (IGH), University of California, Berkeley

Survey preparation and proceedings

Issues were selected for reporting according to what the network partners considered to be the most pressing issues for reform. The issues were arranged in clusters:
- Sustainable financing of healthcare systems (funding and pooling of funds, remuneration and paying providers)
- Human resources
- Quality issues
- Benefit basket and priority setting
- Access
- Responsiveness and empowerment of patients
- Political context, decentralization and public administration
- Health-system organization/integration across sectors
- Long-term care
- Role of the private sector
- New technology
- Pharmaceutical policy
- Prevention
- Public health

If an issue did not fit into one of the clusters, participants could create an additional category to report the topic.

Reporting criteria

For each survey, partner institutes select up to five health-policy issues according to the following criteria:
- Relevance and scope
- Impact on status quo
- Degree of innovation (measured against national and international standards)
- Media coverage/public attention

For each issue, partner institutions fill out a questionnaire aimed at describing and analyzing the dynamics or processes of the idea or policy under review. At the end of the questionnaire, our correspondents give their opinion about the expected outcome of the reported policy. Finally, they rate the policy according to system dependency/transferability of a reform approach.

The process stage of a health-policy development is illustrated with an arrow showing the phase(s) a reform is in. A policy or idea does not necessarily have to evolve step by step. Also, depending on the dynamics of the discussion in a given situation, a health-policy issue may well pass through several stages during the time observed.

Idea refers to new and newly raised approaches voiced or discussed in different forums. *Idea* could also mean "early stage": any idea present but not anywhere near formal inception. In this way, a "stock of health-policy ideas in development" is established, permitting the observation of ideas appearing and disappearing through time and "space."

Pilot refers to any innovation or model experiment implemented at a local or institutional level.

Policy paper means any formal written statement short of a draft bill. Included under this heading is also the growing acceptance of an idea within a relevant professional community.

Legislation covers all steps of the legislative process, from the formal introduction of a bill to parliamentary hearings, the activities of driving forces, the influence of professional lobbyists and the effective enactment or rejection of the proposal.

Implementation: This stage is about all measures taken toward legal and professional implementation and adoption of a policy. Implementation does not necessarily result from legislation; it may also follow the evidence of best practices tried out in pilot projects.

Evaluation refers to all health-policy issues scrutinized for their impact during the period observed. Any review mechanism, internal or external, mid-term or final, is reported under this heading.

16

Change may be a result of evaluation or abandonment of development.

Policy ratings

A second figure is used to give the reader an indication of the character of the policy. For this purpose, three criteria are shown: public visibility, impact and transferability.

Public visibility refers to the public's awareness and discussion of the reform, as demonstrated by media coverage or public hearings. The ratings range from "very low" (on the left) to "very high" (on the right).

Impact: Ranging from "marginal" (on the left) to "fundamental" (on the right), this criterion illustrates the structural or systemic scope and relevance of a reform given the country's current healthcare system.

Transferability: This rating indicates whether a reform approach could be adapted to other healthcare systems. Our experts assess the degree to which a policy or reform is strongly context-dependent (on the left) to neutral with regard to a specific system, that is, transferable (on the right).

The figure below illustrates a policy that scores low on visibility and impact but average on transferability.

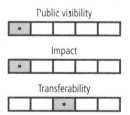

Project management

The Bertelsmann Stiftung's Health Program organizes and implements the surveys, which are conducted every six months. The Deartment of Health Care Management, Berlin University of Technology (TU Berlin), assisted with the development of the semi-standardized questionnaire. We owe special thanks to Matthias Dehn and Sabine Meissner (both with TU Berlin) for their help preparing a first draft of this book, and Kerstin Blum, Ines Galla and Melanie Lisac in the Bertelsmann Stiftung for managerial and editorial support. Special thanks goes to Celia Bohannon for her thorough proofreading.

The results from the seventh and eighth biannual surveys, covering the period from November 2005 to October 2006, are presented in this double issue of *Health Policy Developments*. Of 137 reported reforms, 55 were selected.

Although we describe current developments from the reporting period in detail on our Web site, we chose a somewhat different approach for presenting the findings in this report. Criteria for selection were scope, continuity and presence in public debate during and beyond the reporting period. With this in mind, we looked at topics from the first six surveys independently of their present stage of development or implementation.

Reports from the previous six as well as the seventh and eighth surveys can be looked up and researched on the network's Web site, www.healthpolicymonitor.org. Both these reports and this publication draw upon the partner institutions' reports and do not necessarily reflect the Bertelsmann Stiftung's point of view.

Thanks of course go to all authors from our partner institutions and to those who helped as reviewers and proofreaders.

Authors: Ain Aaviksoo, Tit Albreht, Yael Ashkenazi, Toni Ashton, Netta Bentur, Andreas Birner, Kerstin Blum, Iva Bolgiani, Yann Bourgueil, Shuli Brammli-Greenberg, Karine Chevreul, Janet Clinton, Janet Fanslow, Cathy Fooks, Carine Franc, Gerhard Fuelöp, Ewout van Ginneken, Margalit Goldfracht, Kees van Gool, Revital Gross, Stuart Guterman, Marion Haas, Maria M. Hofmarcher, Phuong Trang Huynh, Wendy Keter, Agris Koppel, Iwona Kowalska, Soonman Kwon, Nicky Liebermann, Miika Linna, Hans Maarse, Faith Mahoney, Esther Martinez, Lisa Maslove, Tom McIntosh, Carol Medlin, Lim Meng Kin, Anna Mokrzycka, Adam Oliver, Karen Pak Oppenheimer, Zeynep Or, Marc Perronnin, Emmi Poteliakhoff, Carol Ramage, Shirli Resnizky, Gerald Röhrling, Michael Rosenbluth, Lacey Roth, Elvira Sánchez, Masayo Sato, Elisabeth Savage, Anke Therese Schulz, Gerald Sirlinger, Elizabeth L. Speaker, Renée C. Torgerson, Sirje Vaask,

18

Lauri Vuorenkoski, Lisa Walton, Cheryl E. Weinstein, Eeva Widström, Laura Wilkinson-Meyers and Nili Ben Zvi.

Comments and suggestions to the editors about this double issue are more than welcome. This series will continue to evolve, change, and, we hope, improve. That is why any input will be helpful.

Reinhard Busse
Sophia Schlette

From idea to implementation

Radical structural reform and development of national health-care systems are the subject of discussion in many countries. However, the road from discussing what should be improved and with what aims, from the actual reform idea to reform implementation, is a long one. In some cases the process is even longer, because of the ensuing evaluation of the reform's effects. Depicting and tracking this journey of healthcare reforms has always been one of the fundamental intentions of this *Health Policy Developments* series and naturally of the Web site *Health Policy Monitor* that undergirds it. However, most reports—both in the books and on the Web site—are mere snapshots of certain steps or stages, as is clearly illustrated by the marks on the arrows indicating the particular reform stage(s). Publication generally occurs on a semiannual basis, thus allowing reforms—or their failure—to be tracked in individual cases. With the Web site's searchable database, users can now also monitor the reform process in certain countries over longer periods of time.

In this chapter, we will present and closely examine four examples of reviewing reform experience over longer periods in the Netherlands, Austria, the United Kingdom, and Finland, thus two countries with statutory health insurance (SHI) and two tax-funded healthcare systems. The four countries serve as an illustration for two questions: Do the two types of healthcare systems differ in their capacity for reform? Do reforms lead to a convergence of the systems, since each type incorporates characteristics of the other (choice and competition are integrated into tax-based systems while central planning is gaining in importance in SHI systems)?

Do reforms lead to system convergence?

SHI countries typically rely on delegating tasks to nongovernmental actors (especially the sickness funds, as well as associations of service providers). The potential for parliament or the government to carry out fundamental reforms is likely to be systematically weaker than in centrally managed systems. At least the Netherlands and Austria confirm this assumption; the reforms, which have now been implemented, were preceded by decades of discussions of the problems to be solved and options for their solution. In both these countries there was consensus about the underlying problem—the fragmentation of the healthcare system—but finding and implementing a consensus about solutions has proved far more difficult and time-consuming.

The original idea behind the 2006 reform in the Netherlands has been around for over 30 years. The year 1974 saw the first quasi-governmental plan to unify the various health insurance systems for acute benefits—the sickness fund system, the private health insurance, and the system for public servants. In 2006, this plan became reality. In the 32 years between, a number of proposals for a "grand" reform were put forward, always met by—partly varying—opposition coalitions around the powerful groups of employers, physicians, and private health insurers. However, numerous smaller-scale reforms were implemented. They can be sorted into two main groups, both of which are pillars of the grand reform that has been implemented. The first is a reform path pursued since the 1980s. It envisioned increased equity in the system by introducing step-by-step reforms within the private health insurance system (e.g., by introducing a basic insurance "tariff") and in respect to accessing the systems (e.g., by integrating self-employed people with low incomes into the sickness fund scheme).

The other path, visible since the early 1990s, calls for introducing elements of market competition, namely the country-wide opening of the sickness funds, the introduction of premium surcharges that vary from one sickness fund to another, and selective contracting between sickness funds and providers. This competition among sickness funds and among healthcare providers was linked to a reduction or elimination of self-governance and a simultaneous increase in government management and supervision. In hindsight, the development resembles a plan by stages—albeit one with many stages and long gaps between them. Although this is of course not the case, it does attest to the persistence of the various government administrations in standing their ground against the critics of the reform.

In the early 1990s, the starting point in Austria for healthcare providers and sickness funds did not differ fundamentally from that of the Netherlands or Germany. The provider landscape was characterized by a distinct separation into outpatient and inpatient sectors with different planning and reimbursement of benefits. Even though the larger sickness funds operated on a regional basis (i.e., not in parallel), a number of parallel sickness funds— for companies, farmers, and so forth—existed (and still exist) that often operate on a national basis, thus creating a situation with a number of funds operating in parallel in each state (*Land*). While Austrians could not (and still cannot) choose their sickness fund, most of the problems associated with the system there resemble those of countries where the insured do have a choice among several sickness funds. The varied risk structure of the sickness funds requires a balancing of funding through a risk-adjustment scheme (which does not exist in Austria) or earmarked subsidies; the need for medical care must be elicited across sickness funds; and planning according to health needs as well as contracting with healthcare providers must either be coordinated among the sickness funds or be left up to the competition among them.

Austria: similar problems ...

Whereas the Netherlands and Germany chose the latter alternative, Austria committed itself to increasing cross-sickness fund planning and management. In 1978, the sickness funds lost their planning and contracting authority in the inpatient sector as a result of the Austrian Hospitals Plan and the national hospital financing budget (which was later regionalized). The original proposal for the 2005 reform then called for expanding centralized management to all sectors. Implementing this idea verbatim would have turned the sickness funds into collection agencies for a national healthcare system—the de facto mirror image of the original proposal for the 2007 reform in Germany, which would have taken contribution collection away from the sickness funds toward one uniform "health fund" while leaving contracting with the healthcare providers in the hands of the sickness funds.

... another solution

Although Austria too has approached its current health system status step by step, the development, unlike in the Netherlands, was not based on an original master plan. Instead, the sta-

States are winners
in dispute between
government and
sickness funds
tus quo of the strong regionalization of the healthcare system
may be seen as a by-product of the conflict between the national
government and the sickness funds. In the federal system, government planning and controlling could only be implemented by
the states, which ultimately assigned a large part of the authority
to themselves through the health platforms created at the state
level.

In contrast, tax-funded systems are considered to be easier for
the government to steer and reform. The examples of the United
Kingdom and Finland attest to this. In the United Kingdom, in
particular, reforms could be implemented quickly, since (time-
consuming) legislative processes are not required, nor do independent actors in the role of payers or purchasers exist in the system. In contrast to the Scandinavian and southern European
countries, where regions, provinces, or municipalities operate
with their own elected parliaments as payers, the National Health
Service (NHS) in the United Kingdom has created separate
health authorities, which have been superseded by primary care
trusts (PCTs). This means that they are not democratically man-
dated to exercise opposition. The greatly varying number of sub-
units of the NHS attests to its power. Some 100 health authorities
were first turned into about 500 PCTs before the number was
again reduced to about 100. This shows the immense freedom
enjoyed by the Ministry of Health and NHS in shaping health
services—and this freedom is fully exploited, as the chain of
reform measures described in more detail below shows.

The situation is different in Finland. There, responsibility for
health care lies in the hands of the municipalities, making the
national government dependent on their cooperation. However,
the decision-making power of the municipalities or provinces is
limited. Denmark has only just implemented an extensive administrative reform (cf. report in *Health Policy Developments*, issues 3
and 4) that transferred responsibility for health care from the
(now dissolved) counties with their own tax-raising competence
to newly created regions without their own taxes. On the basis of
this experience, the Finnish government presented similar proposals to its municipalities in 2005 for the first time. Probably
not by chance, the date coincides with the deadline set for the
municipalities to implement the healthcare reform introducing a

waiting time guarantee. The government's main objective was to eliminate differences other than medically justifiable differences in access to and provision of services.

The Netherlands: Healthcare reform 2006—good things come to those who wait, or intentional salami tactics?

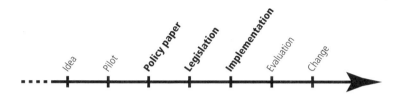

After a discussion that lasted some 30 years, a new health insurance system was introduced in the Netherlands that went into effect on Jan. 1, 2006.

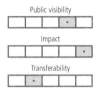

The "Hendriks plan," the first governmental document that proposed a single social health insurance scheme, appeared in 1974. This plan aimed at eliminating the dual division of the Dutch system, which was perceived as a source of disparity in financing and accessibility. The first area of separation was among the various kinds of so-called compartments, namely the Exceptional Medical Expense Act with universal coverage that came into force in 1968, and the systems for "regular" health insurance benefits. The latter, in turn, was separated into the sickness fund scheme, private health insurance, and the insurance scheme for public servants. However, 10 more years were to pass before the first reforms came about.

Basic idea goes back to 1974

These reforms concerned the private health insurance system, which on the one hand, as in Germany, benefited as a whole from the better risk structure of its insured (compared with the sickness funds), but faced the problem of being able to offer insurance to chronically ill and older persons with high incomes only at very high premiums. In order to combat these inequities, legislation was introduced beginning in 1986. On the one hand, a premium supplement (MOOZ surcharge) was collected from all privately insured people, and this surcharge (most recently, i.e., before the reform of 2006, amounting to 10 euros per month)

Private health insurance reforms decrease accessibility problems

was channeled to the central fund for the sickness fund scheme. On the other hand, a basic rate ("tariff") for private insurance was created for all privately insured people who would have been overwhelmed by risk-based premiums. In the Netherlands, in contrast to Germany, legislators made a point of addressing the problem within the private insurance system rather than shifting the responsibility to the statutory health insurance system. The basic rate was subsidized with the help of a second premium supplement. Most recently—before the reform of 2006—the two supplements together amounted to more than 500 euros per year per person insured.

Dekker plan failed, but components implemented step by step Shortly thereafter, in 1987, the Dekker Committee called again for the elimination of the double division of the Dutch healthcare system. It proposed a single income-related insurance contribution with a small additional per capita premium determined by the health insurer. In addition, the proposal called for the possibility of taking out supplementary insurance policies for benefits not covered by the basic insurance. Although the plan was never implemented, in the following years gradual changes were undertaken, primarily in the sickness fund system, which incorporated elements of the Dekker plan. For instance, in 1989, a small additional premium to the income-related contribution was introduced that, starting in 1991, varied from fund to fund. In the beginning, it amounted to less than 10 percent of expenditure, but it later became more substantial. In addition, the benefit basket was redistributed between the Exceptional Medical Expenses Act and the sickness fund system, since the former was supposed to be based on the idea of population-wide planning and the latter on competition. In 1989, all psychiatric benefits were shifted to the "non-competitive" first compartment. Medical devices, prescription drugs, and rehabilitation were also first removed from competition, although they were returned to this compartment later.

Competition versus planning After the change of government, more changes were brought about with the Simons plan. Starting in 1992, these included the free choice of sickness fund, the introduction of a prospective risk-related allocation of funds from the central fund to the sickness funds, and the gradual elimination of the obligation of the sickness funds to conclude contracts with all healthcare providers.

In Germany, the choice of sickness fund and prospective allocation of money (in the form of the risk-structure compensation mechanism) were incorporated into the Health Care Structure Act that same year.

The "grand" reform that called for amalgamating the sickness fund scheme and private health insurance could not be realized for a number of reasons. For instance, physicians feared losing income as a result of adjusted fees, employers claimed that higher contributions for their high-income employees would compromise their international competitive edge, and private health insurers wanted to prevent a loss of autonomy if they were to be included in a system-wide allocation of funds. Thus, a reform could come about only gradually. In 1994 low-income old-age pensioners were permitted to be insured through the sickness fund scheme. In 2000 these rights were extended to self-employed people with low incomes.

Private health insurance and sickness funds becoming more similar...

In parallel, a new adjustment of the balance of power between the state and self-governance was introduced. The latter was eliminated and replaced by two coordinating and supervisory boards for the sickness fund system. Thus, at the start of the new millennium, the essential elements of the Dekker plan had been implemented within the sickness fund system. However, the division into different systems remained, causing the discussion about the grand reform, which had never completely died out, to flare up in 2001, with reports and recommendations issued by several commissions.

While there was consensus about the goal of a single insurance scheme, there was a wide range of ideas about how to finance this system, which can be reduced to the following options: an expansion of the sickness fund system of income-related contributions or a flat-rate premium model. In the end, a combination of the two prevailed. The legal form of the insurers in the single system was also a point of discussion. In this area as well, a compromise with private-law insurers under government regulation was reached.

... and ultimately combined

The new social-insurance legislation aimed at preventing inequity in health insurance protection. Income, age and health status should no longer have a dominating impact on the type of health insurance, the amount of insurance premium or access to

Objectives of the new system

27

healthcare benefits. Elements of the new act are the introduction of a flat-rate premium system combined with an income-related contribution, with a risk-related allocation for all insured people and mandatory insurance for all residents of the Netherlands. The second objective was to contain the costs of the healthcare system and make it more efficient. A boost in efficiency is to be achieved by expanding the authority of the health insurers with respect to independent, selective contracts with healthcare providers and by the resulting higher competition among the health insurers. The third objective of the new system is to increase transparency in comparison to the previous system.

At the core: universal health insurance

Since the new Health Insurance Act (Zorgverzekeringswet, abbreviated to ZVW) came into effect, all residents of the Netherlands must have health insurance. The previous distinction between statutory and private insurance (as well as the separate system for public servants) no longer exists. Independent of income, age, and health status, all residents of the Netherlands age 18 and older pay a flat-rate premium. While this premium varies by insurer, all people insured with the same insurer pay the same premium. The insured may choose their health insurer and may change yearly. This source of funding, which is the focus of national—and international—interest, constitutes only 45 percent, however, while income-related contributions—which must now also be paid by persons previously insured privately—make up 50 percent. Government tax subsidies are an additional source of funding.

The actual health insurance law was flanked by other laws in the reform package, namely the Health Care Allowance Act (Wet op de Zorgtoeslag) and the Health Market Structure Act (Wet Marktordening Gezondheitszorg).

Tax increases provide insurance for low wage earners

Low-income insured can receive a subsidy amounting to a maximum of 400 euros per year for single people and up to 1,155 euros per year for married people. The subsidy is administered by a new organization linked to the tax offices. The subsidy is calculated and granted on the basis of the previous year's income and the current year's expected income.

New health regulatory authority

The Health Market Structure Act lays down changes in the previous structures in the healthcare system. A major element is competition in inter-actor relationships, for example by promot-

28

ing market-oriented contracts between insurers and healthcare providers. Even after the law entered into force, the health insurance market initially continued to be monitored by the Dutch cartel office (Nederlandse Medediningsautoriteit, or NMa). In early 2007, the Dutch Health Authority (Nederlandse Zorgautoriteit, or NZa), created in November 2006, took over this function. As laid down in the health-market structure law, the NZa is the regulatory and supervisory authority.

In November 2004, criticism that was both unexpected and vociferous was expressed by an alliance of employers, private insurance providers, hospitals and associations of mentally ill patients in a joint position paper. In the paper, they expressed their support of the reform in general but expressed fears that the health insurance contributions could increase by 20 percent to 30 percent. In addition, they questioned the limited opportunities of insurers to compete with each other. They also feared rising administrative costs and an increasing complexity of the system.

Unexpected critical reaction shortly before enactment

The professional association of general practitioners criticized certain aspects of the reform, in particular its impact on protection of patient data, confidentiality of general practitioners, access of the population to healthcare benefits, and funding.

Patient organizations supported the reform, seeing in it opportunities for patients, such as greater options for choice. At the same time, they saw risks, for instance with respect to the quality of care and competition. Their lobby made it possible for both employers and patient organizations to contract with insurers.

Support by patients

The Social Democratic opposition did not support the healthcare reform. While it recognized and acknowledged the need for reform, it did not agree with its blueprint. It was especially critical of the modified funding of the system.

Resistance by the opposition

The new health insurance law also stipulated the assessment of the effectiveness and the effects of the law within the first five years of its taking effect. In addition, the risk-based allocation scheme is evaluated annually. The law provides for an evaluation by an international team of experts after two years and again after five years.

Support and assessment of the new law

The transition to the new system has taken place more smoothly than had been predicted by a number of critics. In the first year,

Positive results of the reform

29

the average health insurance contribution was lower than the government had expected and many critics had feared. However, this may be due in part to the fact that in order to gain market share, the insurance companies had calculated premiums for 2006, that were so low that they were not cost-effective. In 2006 the average premium rate was 1,050 euros; in 2007, this rate rose by 9 percent to 1,142 euros. At a rate of 25 percent, the willingness of insured persons to change their health insurer was higher than expected. In addition, the chaos at the administrative level predicted by reform critics has not occurred. The financial problems feared by healthcare providers also have not materialized.

It appears as though the reform is empowering citizens and patients on a general level. On an individual basis, the insured have greater options for choice and must be accepted by any insurer. In line with this, high-income patients with chronic illnesses must no longer be insured with private insurers at high premiums but can be insured at the same rates as healthy patients with all insurers.

Defaulting payer = uninsured? On the other hand, the new law also provided for insurers terminating the policies of defaulting payers for the first time. The list of potential defaulting payers is long. It includes people who are unemployed or illiterate, addicts, and potentially even students, the elderly, and self-employed people. Critics worry that 500,000 to 800,000 people could become uninsured. Secondly, the question of whether the new system sufficiently compensates for groups with lower incomes will remain on the agenda for a long time. Thirdly, the question has remained unanswered of how the insurance providers will deal with huge changes in the number of people they insure. Many problems may arise on the administrative level with regard to financing and form of contract with insurance providers.

More competition = long-term financial sustainability + good quality? In the long term, the salient question arises of whether more competition will contribute to ensuring financially sustainable health care at a high level of quality. In the face of stiff competition, will the insurers actually take the needs of the insured into account, or will they launch into pure price competition for the cheapest premiums?

Many physicians fear that the health insurers will have a growing influence on their medical practice, but the insurers have categorically denied this. One insurer has created financial incentives for physicians who prescribe the cheapest drugs whenever this is possible. This procedure is highly controversial, but so far the insurer has won all the legal disputes it has been involved in.

For many politicians in other high-income countries, the reform of the healthcare system in the Netherlands is a model for their own efforts to bring about healthcare reform. In Germany, the discussion has been influenced by the reform in the Netherlands. That discussion encompasses the inclusion of competition or competitive elements in the healthcare system in order to lower expenditure and boost efficiency. However, the specific pre-reform conditions in the Netherlands and the long, often exhausting road to the present law, which is not yet at the end of its development, must be borne in mind. For instance, the new government has already decided to abolish the controversial no-claim arrangement, which provides for reimbursement of a part of the contribution for insured people who have not made any claims.

Reform in the Netherlands: a model for others?

Sources and links:
Maarse, Hans. "Health Insurance Reform 2006." *Health Policy Monitor,* March 2006. www.hpm.org/survey/nl/a7/1.
van Ginneken, Ewout "Health Insurance Reform in the Netherlands." *Health Policy Monitor,* March 2006. www.hpm.org/survey/de/a6/1.

Den Exter, André, Herbert Hermans, Milena Dosljak and Reinhard Busse. "Health care systems in transition: Netherlands." Edited by Reinhard Busse, Ewout van Ginneken, Jonas Schreyögg and Wendy Wisbaum. European Observatory on Health Care Systems and Policies. Copenhagen 2004. www.euro.who.int/Document/E84949.pdf.
Ministry of Health, Welfare and Sport. *A question of demand.* The Netherlands, 2002. www.minvws.nl/images/broch-question-demand_tcm11-45284.pdf.

Ministry of Health, Welfare and Sport. Health Insurance in the Netherlands. The new health insurance system from 2006. The Netherlands, 2005. www.minvws.nl/images/health-insurance-in-nl_tcm11-74566.pdf.

Ministry of Health, Welfare and Sport. Supplement: The new health insurance system in brief. The Netherlands, 2005. www.minvws.nl/images/health-insurance-system_tcm11-62646.pdf.

Ministry of Health, Welfare and Sport. The new health insurance system in brief. The Netherlands, 2004. www.minvws.nl/images/The%20new%20healh%20insurance%20system%20in%20brief_tcm11-56142.pdf.

Ministry of Health, Welfare and Sport. Transitional arrangements for introduction of the Health Insurance Act and Health Care Allowance Act on 1st January 2006. The Netherlands, 2005. www.minvws.nl/images/transistional-arrangements_tcm11-74568.pdf.

Austria: Structural Plan for Health Care strengthens federal states

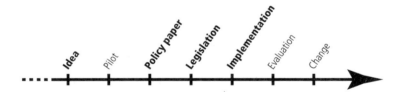

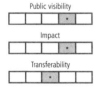

In order to modernize and streamline the Austrian healthcare system, the national government and the states (Länder) developed a concept for restructuring the system and implemented it in 2006. The basis of this restructuring is the Austrian Structural Plan for Health Care (ÖSG), which will be replacing the previous capacity planning in the inpatient sector with integrated capacity planning across all sectors. The ÖSG currently includes only planning of inpatient sector services until 2010. Further, it describes the status quo of service provision in the outpatient sector, the rehabilitation sector and the long-term care sector. The data included in the Structural Plan 2006 for the first time provides an overview of the complete healthcare situation in the various regions, thus allowing the identification of areas with too much and too little provision. This is seen as an important step in overcoming the different regulatory regimes of the sectors. In addition, the Structural Plan forces the federal level, the states and the sickness funds to cooperate.

In Austria, split competencies for planning healthcare provision made a sound foundation for population-wide planning difficult. Moreover, the hospital sector saw cost increases for the sickness funds, which provided about half of inpatient financing. In order to optimize planning of healthcare provision and to be better able to control costs, measures were taken early on. The first Austria-wide hospital plans were developed as early as the 1970s. These plans, however, were not binding. A number of one-off measures targeted at structural policy for coordinated development in the hospital sector brought about results such as a constant reduction in the number of acute beds. This included in particular the establishment of the Hospitals Cooperation Fund (KRAZAF), into which all sickness funds paid and from which the hospitals were financed.

Inpatient sector pioneer for centralization

In the 1990s, the Austrian Hospitals and Major Equipment Plan (ÖKAP/GGP) was developed. In the wake of the healthcare reform of 1997, the government and the states agreed that this plan would be the binding foundation for planning and measures in the acute sector of the approximately 150 publicly funded hospitals. The plan has been updated and expanded several times. Furthermore, the actual funding was transferred to the nine newly created state health funds (not to be confused with the still-existing sickness funds). The heart of the ÖKAP/GGP were binding location rules for hospitals, determination of the overall number of hospital beds and hospitals' specialties, and the maximum number of beds in each specialty ward. The objectives were to guarantee hospital care that was equally distributed throughout the regions and to develop the specialized nature of this care in line with future requirements. From both quality assurance and economic perspectives, the sizes of hospital departments and the range of service related to geographical accessibility were elicited.

Hospitals and Major Equipment Plan

In addition, the expansion of insufficient care sectors (e.g., acute geriatrics, palliative medicine) was pushed and the decentralization and de-hospitalization of psychiatric care spurred. The Major Equipment Plan stipulated the maximum amount of equipment in both the inpatient and outpatient sector with the objective of balancing oversupply and undersupply in the regions.

Objective: to combine planning with quality

The ÖKAP/GGP alone, however, no longer met the complex requirements for efficient and effective management of the healthcare delivery. After some discussion in the 1990s, Austria decided against introducing more competition, as in Germany and Switzerland. It needed therefore to strengthen its planning capacities. In response, the federal government and the states, in accordance with Article 15a of the Austrian federal constitution, determined the joint planning, management and financing, in principle of all sectors, levels and subsectors of the healthcare system, including the interfaces to the long-term care sector for the period 2001 through 2004. For the first time, a link between planning and quality standards was established—but still only for the hospital sector. In 2006, the government and the states finally implemented the Austrian Structural Plan for Health.

The fine line between central regulation and decentralization

Thus, even though it contributes least to hospital funding, the central government has assumed the role of the coordinator and initiator of structural reform over the last 10 years. It has started to develop standards for inpatient care and can impose sanctions on actors not complying. This increased regulatory power came, however, at the price of more autonomy for the nine states which increased decentralization in the Austrian health system. The health reform proposed by the government for 2005 aimed at increasing central coordinating power to all sectors of health care and proposed the establishment of a federal health agency and state health agencies (later renamed health platforms)—thereby attempting to weaken the sickness funds which are dominated by Social Democrats and trade unions. The funds would have de facto lost their contractual relations with the healthcare providers, transferring them to federal and state health agencies.

Health platforms at the state level

Until the end of 2005, the nine federal states had established the health platforms with the objective of taking on overall responsibility for the healthcare providers and the health insurers. These health platforms work closely with the federal health agency,

34

which has also been newly created. A core responsibility of the state health platforms is the coordination and management of outpatient and inpatient care. A second core responsibility is the establishment of interfaces between the two healthcare sectors in order to create integrated healthcare structures. This is to prevent repeated examinations and waiting times (see *Health Policy Developments,* issue 4).

The funds for creating an interface between outpatient and inpatient care are made available in a so-called reform pool. At the outset, funds amounted to 1 percent of the entire funding for outpatient and inpatient care, at about 120 million euros for 2005 and 2006. For 2007 and 2008, the pool is being doubled, to 240 million euros. The funds are primarily used for model projects of integrated care. The analogy to Germany's Statutory Health Insurance Act, which came into force in 2004, cannot be overlooked. **Reform pool for integrated care**

The increased planning of care delivery by the health platforms is intended to define care provision that is need-based on the one hand and are provided under defined qualitative conditions on the other. In the wake of the healthcare reform of 2005, quality criteria were developed throughout Austria that are oriented toward the care level, staff and infrastructural framework, and the minimum frequency of services. The criteria support the goal of cross-sectoral cooperation. From an institutional point of view, the development of quality criteria falls under the scope of the federal health agency. **Quality control**

During the negotiations before the implementation of the reform of 2005, the Ministry of Health, despite enormous opposition (especially by the sickness funds), defended the establishment of federal and state health agencies. It argued that the agencies would not need to be established from scratch, but could be re-established from the existing state commissions, thus precluding any expansion of the bureaucracy. In the course of negotiations on the reform, the sickness funds managed to retain parts of their autonomy in negotiating contracts with providers. They are represented in the state health platforms and even hold the majority vote on decisions regarding the ambulatory sector. During the negotiations, the physicians' chambers also won the right to participate in the health platforms. Despite this achievement, they are not satisfied with the outcome of the reform. The biggest **Ministry pushes through reform despite huge opposition** winners were certainly the states, which have ultimately become the key actors for all of the healthcare sectors.

Position of the physicians' chambers

The Austrian physicians' chambers warn that sickness funds and hospitals follow massive dumping strategies at the expense of physicians engaged in outpatient care. An example cited was the rejection of new colonoscopy examinations as part of preventative medical checkups. The Austrian Physicians' Chamber was not prepared to accept the fee schedule of the sickness funds. In response, the sickness funds made offers to hospitals. Hospitals' marginal costs are lower than those of physicians (in private practice), since the hospitals already have capacities that they want to utilize.

Concerning the reform-pool projects that were set up to promote structural changes, the physicians' chambers pushed projects for financing training and for setting up group practices for general practitioners and specialists. These practices should be the first point of contact for patients outside normal opening hours, thus relieving the expensive outpatient units at hospitals.

While the president of the Tyrolean Physicians' Chamber embraced the increased outsourcing of hospital services to physicians in private practice, he called for more sweeping legislation, such as laws that would permit new forms of cooperation and teamwork among physicians ("physician ltds."). He also called for laws governing the financing of on-call services and institutional long-term care. The Tyrolean Physicians' Chamber president also criticized the dominance of state representatives, sickness funds, and hospitals in the health platforms, while physicians and patients only have one representative each.

Sickness funds support efforts to integrate care

The president of the Lower Austrian regional sickness fund embraced the new health platforms. He particularly supported the search for new forms of cooperation from which physicians would profit as well. One project the president would like to see realized is the disease management program that has already been elaborated by the sickness fund concerning type 2 diabetes. Representatives of the Tyrolean regional sickness fund expect the new organizational structure to prove that physicians in private practice can provide care of the same quality as, but work more cost-effectively than, the outpatient units of hospitals. The representatives of the Tyrolean sickness fund are of the opinion that the success of the healthcare reform depends to a large extent on reform pool projects. Another important aspect is the opening of the hospitals to practicing physicians, allowing them to use facilities such as magnetic resonance tomography or operating rooms.

Despite concessions to the hospitals and states, the reform has proved to be a crucial shift in paradigms for healthcare planning with the establishment of the federal and state health agencies and the development of the Austrian Structural Plan for Health. The conventional capacity planning of the individual subsectors of health care has been replaced by joint single-framework planning based on the methodology of service planning. Thus for the first time, the planning encompasses the entire healthcare system and is being carried out on an integrated basis. The integrative approach has been decisive in setting the direction for shifting services among the various sectors of the healthcare system, for instance, from the inpatient to the outpatient sector. It has established the foundation for implementing healthcare reform in the state health platforms and for the steps to come.

Effects of the reform

Sources and links:
Hofmarcher, Maria M., Gerald Röhrling, Andreas Birner, Gerhard Fuelöp. "Integration of care after the 2005 health reform." *Health Policy Monitor*, April 2006. www.hpm. org/survey/at/a7/1.
Hofmarcher, Maria M., Josef Probst and Romana Ruda. "New rules for preventive health check-ups." *Health Policy Monitor*. October 2005. www.hpm.org/survey/at/a6/2.
Hofmarcher, Maria M. "Austrian Health Reform 2005: Agreement reached." *Health Policy Monitor*, November 2004. www.hpm.org/survey/at/a4/1.
Hofmarcher, Maria M., and Monika Riedel. "The Austrian Health Reform 2005." *Health Policy Monitor*, October 2004. www.hpm.org/survey/at/a4/4.

Bundesministerium für Gesundheit und Frauen. *ÖSG – der neue Weg in der Gesundheitsstrukturplanung.* www.bmgfj. gv.at/cms/site/attachments/1/0/1/CH0037/CMS113698

3382893/oesg_der_neue_weg.pdf [available only in German].

Hofmarcher, Maria, and Herta Rack. *Austria: Health system review. Health Systems in Transition* (8) 3, 2006. 1–247.

Österreichisches Bundesinstitut für das Gesundheitswesen. *Österreichischer Strukturplan Gesundheit 2006 – ÖSG 2006,* Vienna 2006. www.bmgfj.gv.at/cms/site/attachments/1/0/1/CH0037/CMS1136983382893/oesg2006_280606.pdf [available only in German].

Republic of Austria. *Report on Health Care and Long-Term Care,* 2005. http://ec.europa.eu/employment_social/social_protection/docs/hc_ltc2005_at_en.pdf.

England and Wales: Ten years of Labour— more market, more choice in healthcare

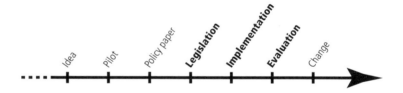

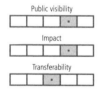

In Britain, the National Health Service (NHS) is considered one of the country's greatest post-war achievements. The principle of equity, which states that medical care must be accessible to all depending on clinical need, not ability to pay, remains as popular and important today as it was when the NHS was established. Despite or perhaps precisely because of this popularity and visibility, the NHS is subject to constant reform.

Preserving the basic principles ...   Upon coming to power in 1997, the Labour government made the reform of the healthcare system one of the central aspects of its political agenda. In the NHS Plan 2000, the government described the aims of this reform, which was meant to preserve the founding principles of the NHS: "universal, comprehensive and free of charge at the point of use." The foremost objective of the reform was to reduce the long waiting times. Further targets

38

were to improve the quality of treatment and to reduce social inequities in access to health care. With its large parliamentary majority and the absence of other legitimized actors, the Labour government easily carried through the individual reform measures during its first two terms in office.

The British government was and is aware that the NHS has not kept pace with social change in all areas of life and that reforms are necessary. Notably, NHS funding has fallen behind that of healthcare systems in comparable countries. The government believes there has been a lack of investment in the NHS in past decades, with the result that patients have sometimes had to wait too long for certain types of treatment and that expectations of health care have not been fully met. With this in mind, the British government in 2000 launched the biggest reform and investment program in the history of the NHS. "The NHS Plan: A Plan for Investment, a Plan for Reform" is designed to equip the NHS for the 21st century.

... but adapting the NHS for the 21st century

One of the ways in which the government achieved a reduction in waiting times was by increasing the health budget from 6.8 percent (1997) to 7.7 percent (2002) of gross domestic product. The previous extremely low health expenditure was to be successively aligned with the average of the EU member states. Funds were largely spent on recruiting more personnel since the waiting times were mainly ascribed to staff shortages. Hospitals and general practitioners in particular benefited from bonuses for providing high-quality care (see *Health Policy Developments*, issue 4).

More money, shorter waiting times

To ensure quality care and to improve the efficiency and structure of the NHS, the government in 1999 established the National Institute for Health and Clinical Excellence (NICE). The task of NICE is to identify geographical barriers to healthcare access and evaluate new technologies. It studies the clinical benefit and cost-effectiveness of treatments, especially drugs, and makes recommendations on their use or non-use to the NHS (see *Health Policy Developments*, issue 2).

NICE sets standards for quality and cost-effectiveness

The Healthcare Resource Group (HRG) system was introduced in an attempt to further shorten waiting times at NHS hospitals and to boost the productivity and quality of services. While the reforms did indeed help reduce waiting times (see *Health Policy Developments*, issue 6), it remains questionable whether the

Higher productivity through healthcare resource groups

HRGs improved the quality of services, owing to the lack of suitable quality indicators and the risk of patients being dismissed too soon.

A further component of the reform is the introduction of performance criteria for hospitals, with the aim of improving productivity. If the criteria are not met, the NHS may dismiss the management of an institution. If they are met, the management is given more decision-making autonomy through the conversion of the hospital trusts into foundation trusts. Management also receives a larger annual budget (see *Health Policy Developments*, issue 4). The star rating of hospitals is meant to make the system more transparent for patients. Assessment is based on waiting times, treatment-related data and the financial management of the hospital. However, experts doubt whether patients are able to make the right choice for their individual treatment on the basis of the data given in the rating.

A further market-oriented element of the hospital reform is to offer patients more choice (see *Health Policy Developments,* issue 3). Their general practitioner now gives them the opportunity to choose treatment at one of four or five hospitals rather than referring them to a specific hospital.

The relationship between the NHS and private actors may provide more food for discussion than NICE, HRGs, star ratings and hospital choice put together. As a first step, the private finance initiative (PFI) was created. In this, private investors build hospitals for the NHS, which leases them for long periods on fixed terms. Recently however, the NHS has also signed contracts with private service providers, in particular outpatient diagnostic and therapy centers. Experts believe that the use of private providers may be more expensive for the NHS than funding new public institutions.

Although the waiting times for treatment of certain indications have diminished in past years, it is not clear whether access to the health system for the population as a whole has really improved. Studies that define morbidity as a requirement, and the use of services as an access parameter, show disparities in access by different income groups, with rising access for more affluent groups. These results run counter to the objectives of the Labour government.

It is also questionable whether upping the budget suffices as the main incentive for improving the NHS. According to experts, the reform measures in the past nine years have not succeeded in modernizing NHS structures. On the contrary, inadequately coordinated individual reforms to introduce free-market elements have done more to undermine the basic principles of the NHS. The positive effect on waiting times is largely due to budget increases, not to modernization of the NHS.

Money alone is not enough

Researchers fear that a larger budget and competition-based reforms may damage the NHS in the long term because its structures have not been fundamentally changed but merely destabilized by free-market elements. As the annual healthcare budget supplements are phased out in years to come, old problems may rapidly resurface.

Core principles of NHS in jeopardy

Sources and links:

Oliver, Adam. "Progress on Waiting Times (April–August 2006)." *Health Policy Monitor,* October 2006. www.hpm. org/survey/uk/a8/4.

Oliver, Adam. "Health care reform in England: progress and plans." *Health Policy Monitor,* April 2006. www.hpm. org/survey/uk/a7/2.

The NHS plan: a plan for investment, a plan for reform, www.nhs.uk/nhsplan.

Department of Health. 2006 – A year of transition, a year of reform. London 2006. www.dh.gov.uk/Publications AndStatistics/PressReleases/PressReleasesNotices/fs/en? CONTENT_ID=4126157&chk=NVWlq%2B.

NHS. About the NHS – How the NHS works. www.nhs. uk/England/AboutTheNhs/Default.cmsx.

Oliver, Adam. "The English National Health Service: 1979–2005." *Health Economics* 14 (Suppl. 1) 2005: 75–99

Finland: Government successfully enforces shorter waiting times

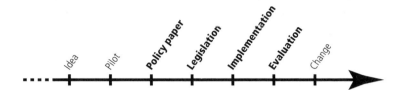

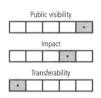

Public visibility

Impact

Transferability

National Action Plan for Health Care 2002–2007

In 2001, rising healthcare expenditure and the problems in providing adequate health services (as evidenced by the long waiting lists in certain parts of the country) reappeared on the political agenda and were underscored by a 10-week strike by public-sector doctors.

Subsequently, the government published its National Action Plan for Health Care 2002–2007 and charged the Ministry of Social Affairs and Health with its implementation. The proposals were to be put into practice in cooperation with regional authorities, municipalities, nongovernmental organizations and other stakeholders.

The Action Plan is very comprehensive and includes the following elements:

1. Ensuring access to treatment: Patients should receive basic health care within a three-day waiting period, be able to see a specialist within three weeks of referral, and generally receive treatment within three to six months.
2. Local services: Local healthcare services should be organized as a functional package at the regional level (see *Health Policy Developments*, issue 3), and provided in association with social services, with interregional collaboration in sparsely populated areas where a larger population base is required.
3. Special health care: Hospital districts should be combined, or their collaboration expanded, to enable them to offer specialized healthcare packages.
4. Structural reforms: The reform of the healthcare system should be undertaken in cooperation with the Ministry of Social Affairs and Health and the Association of Finnish Local and Regional Authorities and phased in progressively.
5. Staff-shortage measures: Medical faculties should increase their annual enrollment of medical students from 550 to 600

students in 2002 to alleviate the current shortage of physicians. Physicians should serve as health-center doctors for a minimum of nine months, and the relevant legislation on training and qualifications should be amended accordingly.

6. Pay systems: These should be replaced by a pay system providing incentives and promoting efficiency.

For many years, access to primary health care entailed long waiting times. These were mainly due to staff shortages at primary health centers and at hospitals in geographically isolated municipalities. In 2001, the government announced (as part of its project to secure the future of health care) that it would redress regional differences in access to health care and improve access for the rural population. A working group of the Ministry of Social Affairs and Health was ordered to draw up proposals to shorten waiting times. The group came up with a mixture of guarantees for access to non-emergency treatment in general and indication-specific treatment.

Focus on waiting times

Patients in need of treatment must be assessed by a healthcare professional within three days of a patient's first contact with a primary health center. In non-acute cases, public hospitals must assess the patient's need of treatment within three weeks of receiving the doctor's referral. Depending on the type of treatment, hospital treatment must be carried out within six months at the latest. If this is not possible, treatment must be arranged elsewhere, either in a different hospital district or the private sector, at no extra charge to patients.

Specification of maximum waiting times …

To solve the problem of a general guarantee that would not do justice to individual cases and indication-related guarantees that would mean that patients with other diagnoses might have to wait longer, 193 guarantees for the most common types of examinations and treatments were defined that cover 80 percent of all non-emergency patients. These are included in specific guidelines based on proposals by experts.

… generally and indication-specific

Faced with the prospect of the national government imposing mandatory stipulations in their own sphere of responsibility, health care, municipalities objected to the new legislation. As opponents, however, they were in a weak position because they could hardly condemn the reduction of regional differences, and

Municipalities against, private service providers in favor

because, as in Denmark, they were at risk of losing their health competencies. Private health institutions, with even less influence, supported the law in hopes of gaining more patients since public hospitals would be unable to stick to the specified waiting times. The legislation on time frames for access to treatment took effect as planned in March 2005.

Evaluation shows clear improvements

The effect of the regulations guaranteeing treatment within set time frames was evaluated for the first time at the beginning of 2006. The evaluation showed that the legally established treatment guarantees had led to substantial improvements in access to primary health care, even if not all goals had been achieved. In February 2006, researchers found, 80 percent of the population lived in municipalities with no problems in accessing primary health care, as against only 37 percent in early 2005. Looking at individual patients, 96 percent received treatment within the set time frame of three workdays, compared with only 49 percent in 2005.

Waiting times halved for specialized medical care

At the beginning of 2005, there were still 41,000 patients who had waited more than six months for specialized medical care. This figure had shrunk to less than 20,000 by December 2005.

Staff shortage remains acute at public institutions

Despite these results, the public health institutions are not satisfied with the reform. They still complain of acute staff shortages and in many cases point to private hospitals that are benefiting from the reform. In the future, the government will have to address the staff shortage at public health institutions, since the transfer of patients from the public to the private sector has not solved the underlying problem.

Sources and links:
Vuorenkoski, Lauri. "Centralizing supervision of health services." *Health Policy Monitor,* April 2006. www.hpm. org/survey/fi/a7/2.
Vuorenkoski, Lauri, and Ilmo Keskimäki. "Ensuring access to health care." *Health Policy Monitor.* April 2004. www.hpm.org/survey/fi/a3/3.

Ministry of Social Affairs and Health. Decisions in Principle by the Council of State on securing the future of

health care. Helsinki 2002. www. pre20031103.stm.fi/
english/eho/ publicat/bro02_6/bro02_6.pdf.

Ministry of Social Affairs and Health. Access to treatment.
www.stm.fi/Resource.phx/eng/subjt/healt/access/index.
htx.

Ministry of Social Affairs and Health. Health Care Services
are improving: Timeframes for access to non-emergency treatment. www.stm.fi/Resource.phx/publishing/
documents/ 3524/index.htx.

Need-based care

Need can be defined as "a condition that, if treated with specific medical measures, can be expected to result in health benefits" (Advisory Council for the Concerted Action in Health Care, 2000/2001). One has to differentiate, though, between need and demand. In this context, demand, also called subjective need, is the subjective desire of an individual for a treatment or benefit. Objective needs arise when a subjective need is confirmed by a medical professional. Objective needs that are not preceded by subjective needs and that lead to no use being made of the healthcare system are also referred to as "latent" or potential needs (Advisory Council for the Concerted Action in Health Care, 2000/2001).

The care provided by a health system is not primarily oriented to the objective need of an individual but to the need of insured populations or defined patient groups—such as all those meeting certain indications. The needs of such target groups may be determined on the basis of epidemiological estimates of the extent and frequency of occurrence of certain diseases.

Need of a target group is relevant

Care services are not need-based if there is overuse, underuse, or misuse. If the services provided go beyond individual needs and there is no indication or insufficient evidence of their (additional) benefit, an instance of medical overuse has occurred. Underuse is characterized by refusing or not providing medical treatment although there is an individual, professional and scientifically proven and accepted need and there are services available at an acceptable cost-benefit ratio. Misuse is health care that causes avoidable damage or the provision of services whose harm or harmful potential clearly exceeds its (possible) benefits (Advisory Council for the Concerted Action in Health Care, 2000/2001).

Need-based care

The goal of need-based care is to arrange health care that meets as well as possible the objective need of the population—that is, the medically established needs for which there are treatment possibilities available. The barriers that can exist between the objective need and the actual demand for a health procedure are also taken as a measure of equity. The ideal state of equity would be reached if everyone with a comparable state of health could access the same health care, irrespective of sex, age, occupation, income, ethnicity or religion (Schäfer et al. 2005: 1495). One aim of the reforms described in this chapter is to reduce this barrier.

As an example, in Israel an innovative, interactive e-learning program for doctors in primary care helps improve health care for women in the Israeli health system (see page 63). A national study from 1998 showed that the Israeli health system did not provide adequate care for women, particularly regarding psychosocial questions and prevention. In addition, Israeli women's state of health is not only worse than that of Israeli men but also worse than that of women in other Western countries. The study demonstrated an objective need for which no adequate care was provided. This is a case of underuse or misuse. A large funding project of the Jewish Association of Cleveland aims to reduce deficits in care for women in Israel. As a subproject, the largest Israeli health insurer, Clalit, developed an innovative training program for doctors in primary care. There, doctors use an interactive e-learning method to learn about topics such as sex-specific health, puberty, menopause, and osteoporosis.

In many countries, care for the mentally ill falls short of the objective needs of the population. We report on approaches adopted in Canada and Israel that aim at eliminating shortcomings in this field. In Canada, the care provisions for mental and addictive illnesses were previously scattered over the country, and many patients did not receive appropriate treatment (see page 56). A national strategy, it is hoped, will improve care and prevent mental illnesses and drug addiction. Another aim is to promote the integration of the various service providers to ensure better care in the long term. In addition, the specific needs of various groups in the population, such as the native peoples, children, immigrants and seniors, will be taken into consideration.

In Israel there are also plans to improve the quality of care for people with a mental illness and people who are suffering from an addiction (see page 59). Care for the mentally ill is not covered by the health insurers in Israel but is provided directly by the Health Ministry. This sector has always been plagued by long waiting times and inadequacies. As a consequence of the dramatic rise in mental illness in Israel, need is also increasing. But the reform process has been stuttering for years. The goal of the reform process now is to transfer responsibility for the care of the mentally ill to the four health insurers (Rosen 2003). One health insurer is preparing for a possible transfer of responsibilities by training primary physicians in the diagnosis and treatment of the mentally ill.

Training course for primary physicians

The health service in Britain has repeatedly been analyzed for inequalities, equality of opportunities and equity. The Acheson report (1998) on health inequalities called for equity audits as a binding part of the planning for the National Health Service. Since then, inequalities for clearly defined population groups in the causes of illnesses, in access to health care and in treatment must be systematically examined. This is in accordance with the principle that individuals with the same characteristics should be provided the same care (Mooney et al. 2002). We present two reforms from England and Wales that aim at ensuring need-based provision (see pages 51 and 54).

Provision of health services based on need in the United Kingdom

The National Institute for Health and Clinical Excellence (NICE) is responsible for the evaluation of technologies. If it reaches a positive verdict, then the technology is binding for the NHS. A goal of the 12th NICE working program is to make effective and appropriate services available throughout the country. In the past, services were provided in some regions but not in others. This "prescription by post code" is to be restricted by the NICE evaluations. NICE evaluations have the goal of recommending the provision of services that are medically effective and economically efficient. If a technology does not meet these criteria, it is excluded from the benefit basket of the NHS. NICE endeavors to make its decisions on the basis of medically and economically verifiable criteria.

NICE limits post-code prescribing

In order to match the supply of care more appropriately to need, practice-based commissioning has been introduced in primary care in England and Wales. The assumption behind practice-

Practice-based
commissioning to
target care to
population needs
based commissioning is that if doctors assume financial responsibility they will provide care that is not only more economical but also better oriented to the needs of the regional population. Savings made are to be reinvested in improving care. The general practitioner retains 70 percent of the savings but can use this money only for his practice and for increasing the range of services that he provides.

Singapore:
Medisave covers
ambulatory DMPs
The organization of payment systems can also lead to misuse in a health system. An example is the lack of flexibility in the use of health savings accounts in Singapore. In the past, health savings accounts could be used only to pay for inpatient care. But that left the chronically ill, which in Singapore account for a quarter of the population, to bear the high costs of ambulatory care. Doctors reported that although there was objective need, patients were not using services or only partly using them because of the financial barriers. To avoid such misuse or underuse by the chronically ill, and thus to prevent avoidable harm, Singapore has introduced ambulatory disease management programs (DMPs) in combination with the financial incentive that money from health savings accounts can also be used for ambulatory care (see page 66).

Sources and further reading:

Acheson, Donald. Independent inquiry into inequalities in health. London: The Stationery Office, 1998.

Advisory Council for the Concerted Action in Health Care. *Report 2000/2001. Appropriateness and Efficiency. Vol. III: Overuse, Underuse and Misuse. III. 3. Need, Appropriate Care, Overuse, Underuse and Misuse.* www.svr-gesundheit.de/Gutachten/Gutacht01/Kurzf-engl01.pdf.

Mooney, Gavin, Stephen Jan and Virgina Wiseman. Measuring health needs. In *Oxford Textbook of Public Health.* Fourth Edition, edited by Roger Detels, James McEwen, Robert Beaglhole and Heizo Tanaka. Oxford and New York: Oxford University Press, 2002: 1765–1772.

Rosen, Bruce. *Health care systems in transition: Israel,* edited by Sarah Thomson und Elias Mossialos. European Observatory on Health Care Systems. Copenhagen 2003.

Schäfer, Thomas, Christian A. Gericke and Reinhard Busse. Health Services Research. In *Handbook of Epidemiology*, edited by Wolfgang Ahrend and Iris Pigeot. Berlin, Heidelberg and New York: Springer, 2005: 1473–1543.

England: Practice-based commissioning for GPs

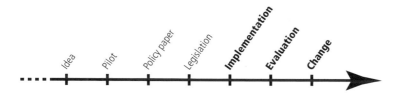

General practitioners (GPs) have a key role in the British health system. As independent contractual partners of the National Health Service (NHS), they provide primary care, but they also purchase—or "commission"—secondary care as local groups of GPs known as primary care trusts (PCTs). Since April 2005 it has been possible for GPs to receive a practice-based commissioning allowance from the PCT. Within the framework of this budget they must not only provide their own medical services but also purchase hospital care.

The doctors are financially responsible for the care of their patients. As an incentive to participate in practice-based commissioning, doctors can retain for their practice 70 percent of the savings made. However, they must invest the retained savings in their infrastructure or in expanding the services that they provide. Budgets must be balanced over three years; that is, the participating general practitioners have financial scope for the use of the available or saved funds. If the doctor does not achieve a balance within the three-year period, he loses approval for practice-based commissioning.

GPs financially responsible

Introduced in the 1990s by the Thatcher government, the practice-based budgets were abandoned in 1997 following the election of the Labour government. Although there are few indications that this policy was successful in the past, Labour reintroduced the budgets in 2005.

Dubious revival

The government expects that practice-based budgets will offer enough incentives to motivate GPs to provide more effective and economic medical care that will also be more suited to the needs of the local population. But the reservations are the same as in previous years. Even if the budgets make it possible to draw on possible short-term profitability reserves (e.g., by general practitioners requesting shorter hospital stays or ambulatory operations and being more careful with the drugs they prescribe), it has not yet been shown that practice-based budgets in primary care lead to savings and better care.

There is a risk that general practitioners will limit the services they provide in order to stay within their budget and garner savings. But there have been no investigations into whether this has happened. A factor arguing against this is that the PCTs and the Healthcare Commission are responsible for monitoring the GPs. So practitioners must reckon with the possibility that they will be subjected to controls.

Outside the government, opinions about the practice-based budget diverge considerably. Critics say that a single GP's practice is too small to be able to purchase services from large hospitals on favorable terms. Others say that the NHS does not have the capacity to draw on economic reserves with budgets at the level of general practitioners. Another argument is that the NHS does not meet the institutional preconditions for market forces to function effectively.

In May 2006 3,454 of 8,433 GPs in England (41 percent) were taking part in practice-based commissioning; by August 2006 the figure was already 74 percent. The incentives seem to be working. In July 2006 it was also reported that, as a result of practice-based commissioning, some PCTs have been able to make savings amounting to £1 million. These savings were invested in a series of new services, including ambulatory clinics for dermatology, diabetes, orthopedics and DMPs, the purchase of new equipment to treat glaucoma, and consultations of PCT doctors with hospital physicians by telephone or e-mail.

The English Department of Health reports regularly on the development of practice-based commissioning. As a rule, though, the official press releases only report the positive developments, for example the savings of PCTs. Scientific reports and articles that allow reliable conclusions to be drawn about the success or failure of practice-based budgets in primary care will only be published in a few years' time. It therefore remains to be seen whether this project leads to a long-term improvement in the efficiency of the NHS and the access to further services in primary care.

Sources and further reading:

Oliver, Adam. "Developing Practice-Based Commissioning." *Health Policy Monitor*, October 2006. www.hpm.org/survey/uk/a8/2.

Oliver, Adam. "Empowering GPs: A return to fundholding." *Health Policy Monitor*, March 2005. www.hpm.org/survey/uk/a5/1.

National Health Service. www.primarycarecontracting.nhs.uk.

Department of Health. www.dh.gov.uk/PolicyAndGuidance/OrganisationPolicy/Commissioning/PracticeBasedCommissioning/fs/en.

Government News Network. www.gnn.gov.uk/environment/fullDetail.asp?ReleaseID=212418&NewsAreaID=2&NavigatedFromDepartment=False.

England and Wales: The 12th NICE work program

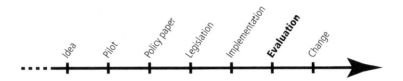

Public visibility

Impact

Transferability

NHS must fund services

Evaluation of education and prevention programs

Broad range of clinical interventions to be assessed

In August 2006, the National Institute for Health and Clinical Excellence (NICE) announced in its 12th work program the technologies it would be evaluating in the coming months. The work plan also stipulates the evaluation of programs that promote public health, especially those targeted at mental health. The objective is to increase the effectiveness and economic efficiency of medical services and programs to promote public health and to restrict "prescription by post code."

NICE is the central institution for Health Technology Assessment (HTA) in England and Wales. Technologies are examined by nearly 60 NICE staff members to determine medical efficacy and cost effectiveness. If the evaluation based on these criteria is positive, the National Health Service (NHS) must provide the respective technologies in all regions and meet the costs. This procedure is intended to counter "post code prescribing," that is, the availability and funding of certain technologies in one part of the country but not in another. Technologies that are negatively assessed can still be prescribed or provided, but a special justification is necessary.

The 12th NICE working program includes the task of evaluating public health programs, such as programs for smoking prevention among children and young people; education in schools about the consumption of alcohol and sexual behavior; advice on physical activity at the workplace, in schools and in the community; and advice in schools and care services about mental health. The growing problem of obesity is also a topic in many of these measures.

Moreover, the 12th NICE work program stipulates the assessment of a broad range of clinical interventions. For example, NICE plans to evaluate idaraparinux sodium for the prevention of strokes, abatacept and retuximab for the treatment of refractory rheumatoid arthritis, alteplase for acute ischemic strokes, and cochlear implants against severe hearing loss.

For the more rapid evaluation of selected technologies, the 12th work program includes "single technology appraisal" (STA), the fast-track appraisal of technologies for individual diseases. This procedure was started in agreement with the government, in order to allow quicker access to technologies and to provide treatment for patients who depend on them.

Shortened evaluation procedures

Whereas NICE is regarded internationally as a model for health technology assessment (see *Health Policy Developments,* issue 2, page 54), in Great Britain there have been discussions marked by controversy after an initial positive reception. NICE's influence on the NHS is thought to be limited. So far, NICE has mainly issued positive appraisals. Politically, it is extremely difficult for NICE to issue negative evaluations, not only because the pharmaceutical industry has a powerful lobby, but also because patients affected by negative decisions (rationing) generate a powerful media echo. And the economic evaluation methods used by NICE are not universally accepted. Nevertheless, the overall goal of NICE is generally welcomed.

Negative appraisals politically difficult

The NHS has a strong interest in excluding ineffective or uneconomical technologies and procedures from the services they provide. However, because most of the NICE appraisals have been positive, there are increasing problems about the financing of the services. Furthermore, in case of negative evaluations, it is the individual doctor facing an individual patient who has to explain that treatment cannot be given. A possible consequence is that patients will take legal action, because the legality of negative NICE recommendations remains unclear. The pharmaceutical industry was opposed to NICE appraisals in principle from the start, because they see in them a fourth hurdle between product development and (funded) care for patients. However, since mainly positive appraisals have been given, the drug manufacturers have benefited from the costs of those drugs having to be borne by the NHS.

Implementation difficulties: not everything can be funded

The Healthcare Commission, a centrally run institution in England and Wales, monitors the extent to which regional NHS service providers apply the NICE evaluations. The NHS has so far followed most NICE recommendations and makes available inter-

Rapid implementation of evaluations

ventions that were positively evaluated. The situation with respect to negative decisions is more complicated, as already mentioned, and a matter of heated debate in the media.

Assessment of public health programs difficult

An open question concerning the evaluation of programs promoting public health is whether there are sufficient and adequate data available regarding the medical and economic effectiveness of these programs. Although there is a good data situation for programs such as for smoking cessation, it remains to be seen on what evidence exactly NICE will base its appraisal of these and other health promotion programs.

Sources and further reading:
Oliver, Adam. "The Twelfth NICE Work Programme." *Health Policy Monitor,* October 2006. www.hpm.org/survey/uk/a8/5.

National Institute for Health and Clinical Excellence. www.nice.org.uk.
Robinson, Ray. "NICE – HTA. External evaluation report published." *Health Policy Monitor,* October 2003. www.hpm.org/survey/uk/a2/1.

Canada: National strategy for mental health

Public visibility

Impact

Transferability

In May 2006, the Canadian Committee for Social Affairs, Natural Sciences and Technology presented a report on mental illnesses that outlined a national strategy for mental health, mental illness and addiction in Canada. The main recommendations of the report involved setting up a permanent commission and a special fund for mental health, with increased research into mental ill-

56

ness, evaluation of programs, and improved access to public services. The strategy should be oriented toward the patient and the family, cover a wide range of topics such as mental health at the workplace, and take into consideration the needs of various population groups such as the native residents, children, immigrants and seniors.

Although mental illness and addiction cost the country some CAD 33 billion (almost 22 billion euros) every year, Canada lags far behind other G8 states in the development of a national strategy for mental health. Care opportunities for mental illnesses and addictions are unevenly spread over the country, and many patients do not receive appropriate treatment. The goal of the measures presented in the strategy paper is to prevent mental illnesses and addictions and to promote the integration of the various service providers in order to secure better service in the long term and to reduce costs of productivity losses associated with mental illnesses.

High costs of mental illnesses

To improve the situation of the mentally ill, the report includes the recommendation to establish a Canadian Commission for Mental Health, which is envisaged as an independent organization. As such it functions as an information center (Knowledge Exchange Centre) for mental health. It would take on responsibility for strategic planning of Canada's services in the field of mental health and addictions and act as coordinator between the various actors in this sector. Other tasks of the new commission are to raise public awareness, receive information about mental illnesses and produce reports.

Canadian Commission for Mental Health

With a new fund for mental health, tax money should be diverted to the regions to improve care for the mentally ill and addicts. Emphasis is on new, affordable and appropriate housing units and rent subsidies for people with mental illnesses. Another important matter is supporting regions as they develop an extensive program to help people with mental illnesses.

Fund for mental health

The new government and the stakeholders support the principles and recommendation of the report for the introduction of a national strategy for mental health. But some groups were critical. They said that there were still major gaps in the report.

A working group for the mental health of women pointed out that the report does not take gender issues into consideration.

Women not considered

The group asserts that the report does not take into account that the majority of patients and of paid and unpaid service providers are women. They also fear that syndromes such as depression and trauma-related illnesses, which affect women in particular, are being forced into the background by illnesses such as schizophrenia and manic depression. There was also criticism that the report has nothing to say about violence against women and neglects topics such as drug abuse and dependence.

Too much emphasis on medical treatment, too little on prevention

The Canadian Psychological Association says that the report could be interpreted from a too traditional viewpoint, with the focus on a medicine-centered system, publicly funded services, and "illness treatment" instead of prevention and health promotion.

Commission evaluates its own activities

It is recommended that the Canadian Commission for Mental Health collect information relevant to mental health and that it make this information available to others. However, since the area of mental health is under the responsibility of the Canadian Health Council, which supervises the overall performance of the Canadian health system, the newly founded commission should not have any powers of supervision of government activities in this field. Rather, the commission should systematically evaluate and report about its own activities to ensure that they are appropriate and effective and that the commission retains its credibility with the governments.

Sources and further reading:

Torgerson, Renée C. "National Mental Health Strategy." *Health Policy Monitor*, October 2006. www.hpm.org/survey/ca/a8/3.

Canadian Psychological Association. *A Review of the Final Report of the Standing Senate Committee on Social Affairs, Science and Technology*, 2006.

Kirby, Michael (Senator). *Out of the Shadows at Last. The Way Forward in Mental Health Reform.* Presentation for the 2006 Thelma Cardwell's Lecture, Faculty of Medicine, University of Toronto 2006.

The Canadian Standing Senate Committee on Social Affairs, Science and Technology. *Out of the Shadows at Last: Transforming Mental Health, Mental Illness and Addiction Services in Canada.* www.parl.gc.ca/39/1/parlbus/comm bus/senate/com-e/soci-e/rep-e/rep02may06-e.htm. 2006.

Israel: Treatment of mental illness in primary care

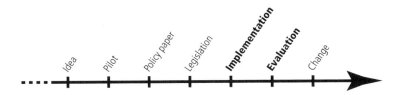

In Israel, the treatment of mental illnesses is not part of the benefit basket funded by the national health insurance scheme; it comes under the direct responsibility of the Health Ministry, which ensures the provisions of services by means of a special budget. As a consequence, long waiting lists and inadequate care exist (Rabinowitz et al. 1999). At the same time, the proportion of adults with mental distress has increased from 28 percent in 1997 to 39 percent in 2005 (Gross et al. 2006). A reform process that has been going on for many years envisages transferring responsibility for the care of mentally ill patients to the four health insurers (Rosen 2003: 125). This should have taken place on Jan. 1, 2007, but has been delayed again by at least six months.

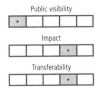

The largest Israeli health insurer and largest provider of health services, Clalit, responded in 2005 in cooperation with a multidisciplinary team by introducing a program to improve the treatment of patients with mental distress in primary care. The aim was to extend the knowledge of service providers about mental distress and to improve their ability to diagnose and treat depression and anxiety conditions.

Clalit seizes the initiative

To reach the targets, obligatory training programs were introduced in 2005 for personnel in primary care as part of a continu-

59

ing education program. In addition, since 2006 Clalit has been distributing guidelines for the treatment of patients with mental distress. Two pharmaceutical companies provided financial support for the development of the training program and provision of equipment.

Clalit hopes that the training program will make for better care and lower costs, in particular for patients with a long history of treatment for symptoms attributed to unidentified mental illnesses. With these measures, Clalit is preparing for the imminent reform and its associated tasks. The incentives for personnel in primary care to take part in the program are not financial; rather, they have to do with the vocational motivation of providing high-quality care and in the insight that the appropriate treatment of patients with mental distress leads to a reduction in the number of visits to the doctor and thus a reduction in the workload.

During implementation of the training program, the following obstacles were encountered:

- Overlap with the implementation of other quality improvement programs (e.g., diabetes treatment)
- Heavy workloads in primary care and short time for each patient visit (7 to 10 minutes)
- Reservations on the part of service providers concerning the treatment of patients with mental distress, due for example to prejudices against mental illnesses
- Shortage of mental health facilities to which patients can be transferred
- High start-up costs for a training program for all personnel in primary care
- Disputes about responsibility for the treatment of mental distress

Clalit carries out an internal evaluation of the program on the basis of structural factors (participation, satisfaction with the training), process indicators (changes in attitudes and knowledge) and results (prescription of antidepressants and benzodiazepines before and after the training).

The evaluation showed that 90 percent of participants thought the training program had been helpful. In addition they felt on average 7 percent better informed and better trained to diagnose

---

Margin notes:

Initiation of training programs and guidelines with support from the drug industry

Improvement in quality, reduction in costs

Handicaps

Internal evaluation

60

and treat patients with mental disorders. To the same extent they perceived fewer obstacles, such as excess work. A constant proportion of 20 percent reported however a lack of self-confidence regarding discussions with patients suffering from depression or states of anxiety. Both the prescription of antidepressants and the defined daily doses (DDD) increased from 2004 to 2005 by 15 percent. The intake of benzodiazepines remained unchanged.

Ninety percent say that they have been better trained

On the basis of the evaluation, the training course was further developed. It now covers three additional units:

Further development of the training program

1. Use of the "mood ruler" (guidelines for the treatment of mental distress)
2. Medication for depression and states of anxiety, and increased patient compliance
3. Coping with the emotional problems of service providers in the treatment of patients with depression and anxiety syndrome

The structural effect of the program is thought to be high because it promotes cooperation among service providers from various sectors in the treatment of mental distress. The training program is also readily transferable; the guidelines and principles of introduction can be adopted for use in other countries with very few alterations. The media in Israel have not yet paid attention to the program because testing and evaluation have not been made public.

Program easily transferable to other countries

It will be possible to evaluate the effects of the program on the quality of care only after a period of four to five years and after the development of indicators measuring the improvement in quality. It is not yet possible to say much about cost efficiency because savings (or a decline in the use of services) has not been observed. However, fairness in care has already increased, because access to health care for mental distress has been considerably improved.

Improvements in quality not yet apparent

Sources and further reading:
Goldfracht, Margalit, Nicky Liebermann and Revital. "Treating mental distress by primary care staff." *Health Policy Monitor,* October 2006. www.hpm.org/survey/is/a8/3.

Bodenheimer, Thomas, Edward H. Wagner and Kevin Grumbach. Improving primary care for patients with chronic illness. *JAMA* (288) 14: 1775–1779, 2002.

Bodenheimer, Thomas, Edward H. Wagner and Kevin Grumbach. Improving primary care for patients with chronic illness: the chronic care model. *JAMA* (288) 15: 1909–1914, 2002.

Goldfracht, Margalit. *Improving mental health care in Clalit Health Care Services.* Abstract for EQUIP conference, Barcelona, 2006.

Goldfracht, Margalit, Ofra Peled, Hanan Munitz, Diane Levin, Chani Shalit, Mireille Danon, Aviv Yaari, Leah Noy, Nicky Lieberman and Dorit Weiss. *Mental distress—knowledge and attitudes of primary care providers.* Clalit health care services internal report 2006 [available only in Hebrew].

Goldfracht, Margalit, Avi Porath and Nicky Liebermann. Diabetes in the community: a nationwide diabetes improvement programme in primary care in Israel. *Quality in Primary Care* (13) 2: 105–112, 2005.

Goldfracht, Margalit, and Avi Porath. Nationwide program for improving the care of diabetic patients in Israeli primary care centers. *Diabetes Care* (23) 44: 495–499, 2000.

Gross, Revital, Shuli Brammli-Greenberg und Ronit Matzliach. *Public perceptions of the health care system.* Myers-JDC-Brookdale Institute Jerusalem 2006 [in Hebrew with abstract in English].

Rabinowitz, Jonathan, Revital Gross and Dina Feldman. Correlates of a perceived need for mental health assistance and differences between those who do and do not seek help. *Social Psychiatry and Psychiatric Epidemiology* (34) 3: 141–146, 1999.

Rosen, Bruce. *Health care systems in transition. Israel.* Edited by Sarah Thomson und Elias Mossialos. Copenhagen: European Observatory on Health Care Systems (1) 5: 2003.

Stern, Ervin, Carlos A. Benbassat and Margalit Goldfracht. Impact of a two-arm educational program for improving diabetes care in primary care centers. *International Journal of Clinical Practice* (59) 10: 1126–1130, 2005.

Israel: E-learning program in women's health

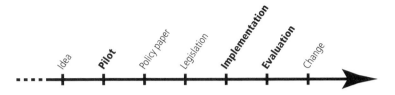

In 2004, Clalit, the largest Israeli health insurer and largest provider of healthcare services, began a pilot e-learning project in two regions to train physicians in women's health. After successfully completing the pilot project, Clalit decided to introduce the program nationwide in all its clinics with three or more doctors. The Clalit e-learning program is part of a major project of the Jewish Association of Cleveland in cooperation with the Myers-JDC-Brookdale Institute to improve health care for women in Israel.

Public visibility

Impact

Transferability

The program utilizes extremely innovative e-learning methods in combination with small learning groups at the workplace. Primary care physicians participating in the program receive on-site training in the various primary care clinics about special questions pertaining to women's health. The course includes topics such as sex-specific health, puberty, menopause and osteoporosis.

Interactive e-learning

The objective is to increase the awareness and knowledge of primary care doctors about the health of women, to raise the doctors' self-confidence and to improve the treatment of women as measured by result parameters. The project also aims at integrating interactive e-learning in the training structures of primary care clinics and to promote on-site learning in working groups. Altogether, these training methods are to improve the effectiveness of Clalit's continuing medical education (CME) within the primary care facilities.

Care specified to women's needs

Doctors above all have an intrinsic interest in taking part in the program because they can develop their professional skills, learn new training methods and benefit from exchanges with colleagues. Other health personnel can also take part in the courses for the same reason. In addition there are external stimuli that can also have an effect, for example the expectations of employers

Motivation for participation

63

and the provision of credit points for participation in the program by various universities and institutes. The doctors also recognize that the program helps strengthen the position of Clalit in comparison with its competitors.

Broad support for the project

The project enjoys support among all the groups involved. The physicians benefit from the professional training and female patients from improved care. The management of Clalit can take advantage of a sophisticated method for CME. Initially, this does involve a high level of investment in the infrastructure and content development, but the training can then be spread widely without major additional costs. Among other reasons, the primary clinics support the introduction of e-learning because the technical equipment will also be useful for other courses in the future.

Main problem is shortage of time

The main problems with implementing e-learning classes in hospitals are the high workload of the personnel and the associated shortage of time, because the courses take place during working hours. A solution could be to provide payments for training sessions after work or to appoint doctors who maintain a clinic's operations while the doctors are learning. But both of these alternatives would involve additional financial resources and are therefore currently not feasible.

Evaluation shows high satisfaction with program

The most important points of both the qualitative and the quantitative evaluation of the e-learning program are participants' satisfaction with the course contents, the benefits of the course, and participants' plans to put what they have learned into practice. More than 80 percent of the participants took part in at least six of the seven course units. In both pilot regions, a high level of satisfaction with the course contents and the presentation of the course material was observed. The acquisition of knowledge was not rated quite as highly but still earned high marks. Almost all participants would recommend the course to others. Most doctors were happy with the method of interactive e-learning and were willing to take courses on further topics. In both regions, the doctors said they had benefited most from the unit on adolescent health.

Increase in level of knowledge

A test before and after the course showed an improvement in participants' level of knowledge about women's health issues. The physicians also felt an improvement in their competence and their confidence in dealing with problems of domestic violence, menopausal symptoms, depression and sexual behavior. The improvements in knowledge about topics such as osteoporosis, lifestyle and eating disorders were not assessed as highly, but these were topics previously assessed as unproblematic. Most doctors either have already introduced changes in the treatment of women or intend to do so. Many see the short time allocated for each patient as the main problem in implementation.

Despite the very different populations and population densities in the two pilot regions, the project was very well received in both regions and the results were positive. This is evidence of relatively high system neutrality, demonstrating that the project could also be applied in other regions and countries. **Program transferable to other regions**

After the evaluation, it can be said that the project has reached its aims in part, for example better knowledge about women's health, increased confidence, and (reported) changes in treatment procedures. The objective of introducing interactive learning methods was also achieved. However, objective data about actual changes in the treatment of women and the influence on their health-related behavior are not yet available. For this purpose, future data for the project will be obtained by surveys of female patients and evaluated together with data about medical indicators.

Although the project has generally been well received, some experts fear that it could also have unintended consequences. Positive effects might be improved health of female patients, leading to fewer contacts with the health system. A negative consequence could be that doctors may want to spend additional time treating psychosocial problems and thus come up against time constraints for patient visits. They would then pressure Clalit to increase the time provided per patient, so that Clalit would in turn have to make more doctors and more resources available. The project could also raise women's expectations, and if time limitations keep doctors from meeting them, frustration and dissatisfaction with doctors and health insurers may ensue. **More staff needed?**

Sources and further reading:

Gross, Revital, Yael Ashkenazi, Nili Ben Zvi, Michael Rosenbluth, Cheryl E. Weinstein, Lacey Roth and Wendy Keter. "On site e-learning for training physicians." *Health Policy Monitor*, October 2006. www.hpm.org/survey/is/a8/5.

Ashkenazi, Yael, and Revital Gross. *Evaluation of ISHA pilot in Clalit Health Services Central district. Findings from post course questionnaires and analysis of pre–post changes.* Jerusalem: Myers-JDC- Brookdale Institute, 2005.

Ashkenazi, Yael, und Revital Gross. *Evaluation of ISHA pilot in Clalit Health Services Northern district. Findings from post course questionnaires and analysis of pre–post changes.* Jerusalem: Myers-JDC-Brookdale Institute (internal document, not published), 2006.

Rosenbluth, Michael. *Proposal for a training program in women's health for primary care physicans in Clalit Health Services* (internal document, not published), 2001.

Singapore: Outpatient DMPs for the chronically ill

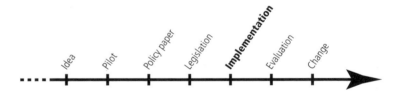

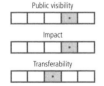

To improve the quality of health care in Singapore, health savings accounts under the Medisave program can now be used for outpatient treatment of chronic disorders within the framework of disease management programs (DMPs). A million patients (a quarter of the population of Singapore) are affected by a chronic disease. The objective is to reduce the medical and financial burdens of lifelong treatment and to establish control of chronic illnesses at an early stage.

In October 2006, the Health Ministry introduced structured-treatment programs for diabetes mellitus and in January 2007 for high blood pressure, lipid disorder, and stroke. There are evidence-based guidelines for treating these disorders and result parameters to check the success of treatment. Patients taking part in the programs can use their Medisave health savings—which in the past were only available for treatment in hospital—for outpatient care (also see page 109).

Structured treatment programs

The starting point of the debate was the insight that costs for ambulatory treatment can lead to financial problems for patients, above all for the chronically ill, because patients were formerly not allowed to use money from their health savings accounts for outpatient treatment. As a result, patients delay necessary treatments or do not comply with medication regimes. Consequences include not only a threat to the therapy's success, but also a long-term worsening of the state of health and a rise in treatment costs. Therefore, allowing patients to use Medisave accounts for outpatient care was chosen as an instrument to limit the financial burden on the chronically ill and ensure the success of therapy.

Strong financial disincentive to use outpatient care

Chronically ill patients enrolled in a DMP now have the opportunity to withdraw up to SGD 300 from their Medisave account each year for outpatient treatment. They can also draw on one or all accounts in the family (spouse, children, parents) for up to SGD 300 annually for each account (up to 10 accounts). The patients will still have to pay a deductible of SGD 30 and a co-payment of 15 percent of the balance after payment of the deductible. The rest is charged to the Medisave account.

Conditions for Medisave use

The project brings with it an upgrading of general medicine. General practitioners can register for the care of the chronically ill. The precondition is that they take part in special training courses. So far 150 GPs have enrolled in the training courses. This number is to be increased to 2,000 eventually. The aim here is to persuade the population that they are in good hands with the general practitioners and that a transfer to a specialist is not always necessary. Hospitals are encouraged to transfer patients to a registered general practitioner for post-hospital treatment. These measures are to help keep down treatment costs, make treatment of chronic disorders better coordinated and enhance the reputation of general medicine.

Upgrading of general medicine

A survey by a daily newspaper showed that 69 percent of those questioned thought that the withdrawal from the Medisave account of SGD 300 was too low. The deductible of SGD 30 was thought by 76 percent to be appropriate. The Health Ministry responded that in the future the withdrawal limit would be reviewed to take inflation into account. In addition, other chronic diseases for which there are recognized treatment guidelines, such as asthma, may be included in the system at an appropriate time.

The introduction of DMPs and the extended use of health savings for ambulatory care of the chronically ill will have considerable implications on service providers, healthcare funding, quality of care, and accessibility of necessary treatment. The coordination of various actors will be improved. Media coverage is extensive, because a quarter of the population and all general practitioners are affected. Daily papers report about patients who are consciously keeping their health expenditures low to save money and who are therefore grateful that in the future they will be able to use their health savings accounts for ambulatory care as well. General practitioners are concerned, though, that if only some of them are involved in the DMP programs, a two-class system of GPs could result.

Patients and associations are asking that Medisave be extended to cover all ambulatory treatment or specific cost-intensive procedures such as MRT. But the government is worried that the savings would quickly be exhausted and would not be adequate for possible future hospital treatment. This worry underlies the limitation to the treatment of chronic diseases and the introduction of deductibles and co-payments. In addition, officials worry that doctors could abuse the system at the cost of the patients or their Medisave accounts by offering unnecessary treatments. Regular examinations will be carried out to prevent this. Other critics draw attention to the fact that an advance deductible of SGD 30 can be a considerable financial burden for many people.

Sources and further reading:

Lim, Meng Kin. "Medisave to cover cost for outpatient chronic care." *Health Policy Monitor*, October 2006. www.hpm.org/survey/sg/a8/5.

Lim, Meng Kin. "Liberalization of Medisave Use." *Health Policy Monitor*, April 2006. www.hpm.org/survey/sg/a7/2.

Lim, Meng Kin. "Disease Management." *Health Policy Monitor*, April 2006. www.hpm.org/survey/sg/a7/3.

Ministry of Health. Medisave for Chronic Disease Management Programme. www.moh.gov.sg/corp/financing/medisave/chronicdisease.do.

Ministry of Health and Health Promotion Board. Chronic Disease Management. www.hpb.gov.sg/chronicdisease/.

Access to the health system

In most highly industrialized countries, access to health care is regarded as a basic right. For example, Article 35 of the Charter of Fundamental Rights of the European Union states that "[e]veryone has the right of access to preventive health care and the right to benefit from medical treatment under the conditions established by national laws and practices."

However, the concept of access to health care needs to be clarified. It can contain various dimensions and can relate, for example, to access to care from a geographical perspective (accessibility of hospitals, doctors, etc.; cf. Alber and Kohler 2004: 23–34) or the access patients have to certain medical professionals, for example general practitioners or specialists (see Rothgang et al. 2005). Studies often select just one of these dimensions and analyze it in depth. **Access to health-care a multidimensional concept**

Here we describe six dimensions of access to health care, which can also be viewed as barriers to access (see Fig. 1; cf. Busse et al. 2006; Wörz et al. 2006). These barriers must be removed if access to health care is to be ensured. At the same time, the access dimensions identified can help locate the reform measures described in this chapter with respect to access.

The first dimension is whether there is universal health insurance coverage (or what the proportion of the population with health insurance is). In most European countries, there are public health insurance systems under which the great majority of the population is insured. **Proportion of population with insurance coverage**

The United States is the only highly industrialized country with considerably less than 100 percent coverage for its population. There are regular reports of about 40 million people, or 16 percent of the population under 65 years, without health insurance.

Fig. 1: Potential access barriers to healthcare

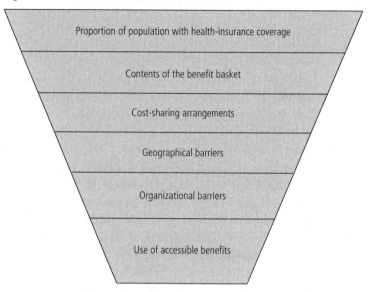

Source: Wörtz, Foubister and Busse, 2006.

To provide adequate medical care, some states are endeavoring to improve access for the uninsured to health benefits and drugs and to make it more affordable. In California, for example, a new law requires pharmaceutical companies to offer cheaper medication for uninsured low-earners (see page 84).

Contents of the benefit basket
Another dimension of the concept of access is the contents of the benefit basket. This determines the benefits to which there would theoretically be access. In many European countries, there has been a trend in recent years to exclude dental care from state or statutory baskets. There have also been opposite tendencies. In 2000, for example, Finland extended access to state-financed dental care to cover all age groups. This reform has now been evaluated (see page 75). Reforms regarding the first two dimensions— or barriers—are further explored in the following chapter on "Health and long-term care insurance".

Co-payments for patients
Some barriers to access are static, others dynamic. For example, health insurance coverage and benefit baskets usually evolve gradually; they rarely undergo radical reforms. Co-payments, the third barrier, are much more dynamic. They are more frequently

changed in the course of revisions to health policies. This is also apparent in this issue of *Health Policy Developments*. Three of eight reform initiatives reported in this chapter describe reform initiatives relating to co-payment regulations for medical benefits. However, there is no uniform international trend in these developments. For example, in Japan the co-insurance rates for the elderly for ambulatory and inpatient benefits were set equal to those for other age groups, that is, they were increased (see page 77). In New Zealand, by contrast, reform initiatives were aimed at reducing co-payments for GP visits (see page 78), and in Singapore the co-payments for stays in hospital were also reduced (see page 80).

Geographical barriers

Geographical barriers are a fourth barrier to health care. This can cover the accessibility of providers of health care, for example the distance to hospitals and general practitioners. Within a country, this primarily affects remote places such as islands, but such barriers are also encountered in rural areas. Geographic barriers are fairly static and can only be influenced to a limited extent by health reforms. We report about corresponding reform initiatives in the chapter "Coping with future shortages of health professionals".

Organizational barriers

Even when health insurance provides a patient with certain benefits, co-payments are moderate, and adequate service providers are geographically accessible, the organization of the provision of health care and the health insurance can favor or impede the (appropriate) access to care. This is apparent in Australia, where the coexistence of state and private health insurance leads patients to make use of inpatient benefits when ambulatory treatment would be more appropriate (see page 82).

Use of accessible benefits

The final access dimension is the basic difference between the accessibility of a benefit and its actual use. In the United States, early experience with health savings accounts indicates that the holders delay necessary treatments in order not to draw on their savings too soon (see page 86). This example also shows that the boundaries between the six barriers to access described here are not rigid, and it is not always possible to make exact distinctions between them. The links between co-payment barriers and organizational barriers are evident.

To reduce costs and raise the quality of care, many countries now have initiatives to exercise greater control over the use of benefits. For example, the Center for Medicare and Medicaid Services (CMS) in the United States publishes regional price data for various elective operations (see page 91). However, the success of this measure is debatable because the prices for individual providers are not published. In addition, no information is provided about the quality of care.

Sources and further reading:
Alber, Jens, and Ulrich Kohler. *Quality of life in Europe. Health and care in an enlarged Europe.* Dublin: European Foundation for the Improvement of Living and Working Conditions, 2004.

Busse, Reinhard, Markus Wörz, Thomas Foubister, Elias Mossialos, Philip C. Berman et al. *Mapping Health Services Access. National and Cross-Border Issues (HealthAC-CESS). Final Report, November 2006.* www.ehma.org/_fileupload/File/HealthACCESS/HealthAccess_Final Report_20Nov.doc.

Rothgang, Heinz, Mirella Cacace, Simone Grimmeisen and Claus Wendt. The changing role of the state in healthcare systems. *European Review* 14 (suppl. 1) 2005. 187–212.

Wörz, Markus, Thomas Foubister and Reinhard Busse. Access to health care in the EU Member States. *Euro Observer* (8) 2: 1–4, 2006. www.euro.who.int/observatory/Publications/20020524_29.

Finland: Better access to dental care for adults

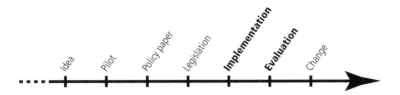

In 2000, the Finnish government did away with age limitations for access to public dental care. In addition, state subsidies for private basic dental care were extended to all age groups. Finnish local authorities, which are responsible for the organization and provision of health services, now have to ensure that all their residents have basic dental care. They can offer benefits themselves or commission other local authorities or private services to provide them. People who make use of private dental benefits are entitled to claim a refund of the costs from public health insurance.

The reform led to an increase in the demand for public dental services among adults. Figures published by the National Research and Development Centre for Welfare and Health (STAKES) and the national social insurance institute show that in 2000, 21.6 percent of adults made use of public dental services. In 2004, 23.5 percent made use of them. In comparison, the percentage of persons 17 and younger making use of the public dental services in the same period remained constant at 76.2 percent. The number of people reclaiming the cost of private dental treatment more than doubled, from 11.5 percent in 2000 to 24.6 percent in 2004. The overall costs for dental treatment in Finland increased in this period by 19 percent.

Increased demand for dental benefits

Large towns and cities, where the public dental facilities had treated relatively few adults in the past, found it difficult to cope with the rising demand. There were long waiting lists, despite a 10-percent increase in staff at the public dental surgeries. Some local authorities are facing a shortage of dentists, partly because the number of students declined in the mid-1990s, and also partly because of the number of dentists now reaching retirement age. The transfer of tasks to dental hygienists was therefore an important additional instrument in the implementation of the reform.

Shortage of dentists makes it difficult to implement reform

Nevertheless, at the end of 2005 about 20 percent of all local communities were still not in the position to implement the reform plans and provide basic dental care to the rising numbers of patients.

Private dental services fear loss of business The private dentists are mostly opposed to the reform. They consider the reimbursement rates offered by the public health insurance too low. In addition, they worry about an increase in competition between the sectors.

Reform improves access Overall, access to dental care has improved slightly. The number of adults treated by the public dental service and the number of people reimbursed for private dental benefits increased. There were noticeable improvements in dental care in acute cases. However, the overall increase in use of dental care was not as great as the government had expected from this reform.

Sources and further reading:
Widström, Eeva. "Extension of publicly funded dental care to all." *Health Policy Monitor*, October 2006. www.hpm. org/survey/fi/a8/2.

Suominen-Taipale, Liisa, and Eeva Widström. Hammashoitouudistus ja hoitopalvelujen käyttö ja sisältö terveyskeskuksissa. *Sosiaalilääketieteellinen Aikakauslehti* (43) 2006. 134–145 [Treatments provided in the Public Dental Services before and after a major health political reform. *Journal of Social Medicine*—abstract in English].

Vesivalo, Arto, Eeva Widström, Hennamari Mikkola and Tiina Tampsi-Jarvala. Terveyskeskusten hammashoidon tavoitteet ja kannusteet hammashoitouudistuksen implementoinnissa. *Sosiaalilääketieteellinen Aikakauslehti* (43) 2006. 146–156 [aims and incentives in the implementation of Finnish dental care reform in the Public Dental Service. *Journal of Social Medicine*—abstract in English].

Widström, Eeva. Oral health care. In *Health in Finland*, edited by Seppo Koskinen, Arpo Aromaa, Jussi Huttunen and Juha Teperi. Helsinki: National Public Health Institute KTL, 2006: 140–141. www.ktl.fi/hif/hif.pdf.

Widström, Eeva, and Liisa Suominen-Taipale. Aikuisten hammashoito terveyskeskuksissa vuonna 2003. *Suomen Hammaslääkärilehti* (15) 2006. 810–814 [adults' oral health care in the Finnish Public Dental Service in 2003. *Finnish Dental Journal*—abstract in English].

Japan: Increased cost—sharing for the elderly

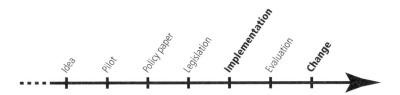

In October 2006, the co-insurance rates for patients above 70 years of age with an income above a certain threshold were increased to 30 percent. The annual income threshold was set at 5.2 million yen (about 33,000 euros) for married couples and 3.83 million yen (about 24,000 euros) for people living alone. The level of co-payments remained at 10 percent for people above 70 with an income below the threshold.

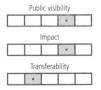

The main aim of the reform was to equalize cost-sharing for medical benefits for people with the same income levels, irrespective of their age. This reform is only one of a series of measures that have successively increased the co-insurance rates for people over the age of 70 from almost zero to 30 percent. As in many other industrialized countries, expenditure on medical care for the elderly has increased steadily in Japan in recent years. In 2006, the costs for this age group accounted for 40 percent of overall healthcare expenditure and caused financial difficulties for some health insurers.

Increasing expenditure for medical care of the elderly

Japan has one of the most rapidly aging societies in the world. The World Bank estimates that the numbers of people over the age of 65 will increase from about 20 percent today to almost 29 percent in 2030 (World Bank 2007). Healthcare costs for this group will increase proportionately. In view of these developments, new

Higher co-payments unavoidable in the future?

financial models seemed unavoidable if comprehensive health care were to be maintained in the future for the entire population.

Sources and further reading:
Sato, Masayo. "Increase of Co-Payment Rates for Elderly." *Health Policy Monitor,* October 2006. www.hpm.org/survey/jp/b8/2.

World Bank. Demographic Projections for Japan. Health, Nutrition and Population Statistics. http://devdata.worldbank.org/hnpstats/HNPDemographic/year5/JPN_POP.xls.

New Zealand: Lower co-payments for visits to general practitioners

Public visibility

Impact

Transferability

The New Zealand health service is largely state-financed. In primary case there is a division between the body administering the public funds for health and the providers of healthcare services ("purchaser-provider split"). The latter are mostly private, and may be either nonprofit or for profit. The first contact with the health system is usually through the general practitioner, an emergency center or an independent nurse. Co-payments for care provided by the family doctor used to range between NZD 35 and NZD 65 (corresponding to 18 to 34 euros). The general practitioners can determine the level of the co-payment independently. Specialist care is provided in hospital and is free of payment (Bramhall 2003).

The New Zealand government has continuously increased the subsidies it provides for GP visits in recent years with the objective of reducing co-payments for patients. The July 2006 phase of this reform process, which increased the support payments for visits to general practitioners by people 45 to 64 years old, was linked with the provision that the general practitioners should give notice of any increases in co-payments. In addition, the government increased the subsidies for GP surgeries that demand lower co-payments from their patients.

More public funds, lower private co-payments

Patients welcome the increased public subsidies for GP visits and the resultant reduction in co-payments (to around NZD 30 or less). The majority of doctors also supported the measures, which are intended to ease patients' access to general medical care. However, the requirement that all general practitioners who receive public subsidies give notice of any increase in their co-payments met resistance. In the future, doctors' surgeries that demand disproportionately high co-payments from their patients are to be referred to an examination board. The board will examine the level of the co-payments and, if appropriate, impose a reduction. Surgeries with low co-payment levels, by contrast, welcome the reform. They are mostly in socially disadvantaged areas.

Increased support payments meet with positive reactions

The reform will increase social equality within the system, because it will make it easier for low earners to use medical services offered by general practitioners. In addition, the government hopes there will be savings, because in the future more people will probably go to their general practitioner first rather than to the emergency services, which actually generate higher costs but for which the patients do not have to pay anything. It is also expected that people will contact the general practitioners at an earlier stage, making health care not only less expensive but also potentially more effective.

Better access for low earners

Sources and further reading:
CHSRP, University of Auckland. "Reducing copayments for general practice (2)." *Health Policy Monitor*. October 2006. www.hpm.org/survey/nz/a8/1.

Bramhall, Stuart. *The New Zealand Health Care System*. www.pnhp.org/news/2003/january/the_new_zealand_heal.php.

Hodgson, Pete. $43 million invested in high needs practices. www.beehive.govt.nz/Print/PrintDocument.aspx? DocumentID=26910.
www.moh.govt.nz/moh.nsf/0/ec272299eccbf6e1cc256c
4f00028d15/file/cabinetpaperlowcostaccess.pdf.

Singapore: Reform of Medishield high-risk insurance

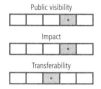

Public visibility

Impact

Transferability

Medishield, a state-administered insurance program for high hospital costs, receives its funds from an age-dependent per capita premium. In addition to the premiums and co-payments, those insured by Medishield pay a certain proportion of the hospital costs themselves. Together with private high-risk insurance, this insurance covers 7 percent of healthcare expenditures. In Singapore, the proportion paid by private households in 2000 amounted to 43 percent of overall healthcare expenditures, a very high percentage (Schreyögg and Lim 2004).

Patients who have to stay in hospital can choose among various standards. Public hospitals usually offer five classes of room, which vary in comfort and in the number of beds. Class A is a single room fitted out to hotel standards (i.e., with air conditioning and television). The patient pays the full cost for this class. Class B1 offers a two-bed room with air conditioning and is 20 percent subsidized. Class B1+ beds are in a four- to six-bed room with air conditioning; 50 percent of costs is subsidized. Class B2 corresponds to class B1+, but with only fans instead of air conditioning. These rooms receive a 65 percent subsidy. Class C consists of wards with more than 10 beds and only fans, with a subsidy level of 80 percent (Schreyögg and Lim 2004).

Lower co-payments for Medishield   Until July 2005, patients drawing on Medishield for their hospital stay had to pay, on average, 60 percent of the invoice out of

80

pocket. After the fundamental reform introduced in 2005 by the health ministry in Singapore (cf. Lim 2005), which mainly involved increases in the per capita premium and the services offered, the private cost share has fallen from 60 percent to 40 percent. In addition, private health insurance programs appeared on the market offering products with Medishield as an integrated part—although with higher contributions from patients who have treatment in a private hospital, namely SGD 3,000 (1,500 euros), compared with $1,000 (500 euros) in public hospitals for a class C bed and $1,500 (750 euros) for class B2.

Medishield now reimburses a higher proportion of hospital costs. In addition, there are more hospital policies to choose from: five insurance companies now offer 18 different tariffs, in contrast to the former three companies and nine tariffs. Nevertheless, the health ministry views the current contribution level (40 percent) as still too high and is working toward lowering it to 20 percent.

Share of Medishield should increase further

Sources and further reading:
Lim, Meng Kin. "Medishield Refinements on the cards." *Health Policy Monitor*, October 2006. www.hpm.org/survey/sg/a8/3.

Schreyögg, Jonas, and Meng Kin Lim. Health Care Reforms in Singapore. Twenty Years of Medical Savings Accounts. *CESifo DICE Report* 3: 55–60, 2004.
Lim, Meng Kin. "Upgrading family medicine." *Health Policy Monitor*, October 2005. www.hpm.org/survey/sg/a6/4.

Australia: More private health insurance products

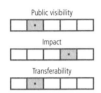

Public visibility

Impact

Transferability

Australia's healthcare system is largely funded through taxation, both general taxation and targeted levies for Medicare. The universal state health insurance offers patients subsidized access to doctors, free treatment in public hospitals and subsidized medication. Private health insurance companies offer additional policies to cover the costs of treatment and stays in hospital as a private patient, fees not covered by Medicare, and additional health benefits such as dental care and medical aids. Private health insurance companies therefore extend the choice for patients and make it possible, against the background of longer waiting lists for hospital treatment, to obtain quicker access to inpatient benefits (Healy et al. 2006).

Private health insurance provides wrong incentives

Since 1984, private health insurance companies have not been allowed to offer insurance products that cover the costs for outpatient treatment, including the co-payments arising within the framework of Medicare (Healy et al. 2006: xvi, 59). This provision has had an unwanted result. Many patients with private insurance demand treatment in the hospital, although there are more efficient, more cost-effective and more appropriate ambulatory alternatives. For this reason, the government plans to revoke the regulations from 1984.

Extending private insurance to outpatient care

As of April 2007, private health insurers can once again offer additional packages that also cover services provided in the ambulatory sector. With a greater choice of insurance packages, patients can choose the product that suits their care requirements.

Changes in the healthcare structures

Another motive for the reform plans in the private health insurance market is the rigid segmentation of the Australian health system. In the past, artificial distinctions were drawn between outpatient and inpatient care. The Australian government has meanwhile recognized that such healthcare structures are no longer appropriate for modern, efficient, high-quality care. They therefore argue that reforms that break down these artificial barriers would lead to better and more efficient care.

The main target group for the new insurance coverage is people with chronic illnesses such as kidney disease and cancer. Patients could then choose whether to have dialysis treatment or chemotherapy, for example, as an inpatient or an outpatient. However, there is also the risk that the chronically ill will have to pay more in the future for such services. In the past, private health insurance was financed by risk-independent premiums (the same premium for all insured persons, independent of age and health risk). Benefits such as chemotherapy have been included in the insurance package even if patients can only use them as an inpatient. Depending on how the private insurers put together these insurance packages in the future, the chronically ill may have to purchase an additional policy to cover such health care—which would effectively be a risk-adjusted premium.

Higher premiums for the chronically ill?

To protect individual private insurance companies against high costs for the care of many chronically ill customers and to provide incentives to insure the chronically ill, the government is planning alterations to reinsurance provisions. Previously, private insurers could only reinsure against the risks of the "elderly insured." This reinsurance coverage is now to be extended to include costs for treatment of the chronically ill. The government hopes to avoid insurance companies having to face financial disadvantages if they insure more elderly and chronically ill people than other insurance companies do.

New reinsurance possibilities for private insurers?

Since the details of the reform have yet to be finalized, it is not possible to predict its effects on the quality and efficiency of care, on insurance premiums and on the financial situation of the health insurance companies.

Private health insurance companies and private hospitals support the reform. Consumer associations are also generally in favor of it. However, they emphasize the need to ensure that outpatient services are at least of the same standard as inpatient treatment and that they achieve the same or better clinical results.

Reform proposals meet with approval

Sources and further reading:
van Gool, Kees. "Private Health Insurance: more products."
Health Policy Monitor, October 2006. www.hpm.org/sur
vey/au/a8/2.

Healy, Judith, Evelyn Sharman and Buddhima Lokuge.
Australia. Health System Review. *Health Systems in
Transition,* (8) 5 2006. 1–158.
Australian Government, Department of Health. Private health
insurance—for consumers. www.health.gov.au/phi.
Consumers' Health Forum of Australia. Private health in-
surance reforms. Consumers have a say. September 2006.
www.chf.org.au/Docs/Downloads/Consumer_Key_
Issues_Paper_Aug_06.pdf.

United States: Reduced prescription-drug prices for Californians without health insurance coverage

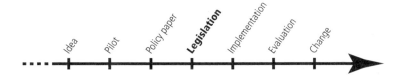

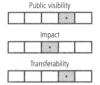

In the United States, some 45 million people, or about 16 percent of the population under 65 years, have no health insurance. In California, 19 percent of residents are not insured. In the past two years, there have been several attempts in that West Coast state to make prescription drugs more accessible to middle-income people who lack health insurance. In October 2006, the legislature finally passed a law that requires drugs manufacturers to make more favorably priced drugs available to some 6 million Californians without health insurance.

The pharmaceutical companies will have three years to put the price reductions in place. The annual income of those entitled to this benefit must not exceed triple the federal poverty level (about USD 60,000 or almost 47,000 euros for a family of four). Californians with exorbitantly high health expenses and Medicare recipients who are not insured for medication costs are also entitled to the price reductions. Drug manufacturers who fail to comply with the reform program will face financial sanctions: Their products will no longer be purchased by Medi-Cal, California's health insurance for the needy. Medi-Cal spends more than $2 billion annually on medications.

Drugs manufacturers must allow price rebates

Gov. Arnold Schwarzenegger originally opted for a different plan involving voluntary undertakings from the drug manufacturers. In July 2006, however, he changed his mind and supported the Democrats' proposal to wield the state's bargaining power to induce manufacturers to offer reduced prices. The Republicans in the state Legislature voted against the reform, asserting that it undermined free-market pricing and voicing concerns that people who had no legal right of residence would be able to benefit from the price reductions.

Governor supports state intervention

The pharmaceutical companies and their associations oppose the reform. They support the failed reform initiative of 2005, which called for voluntary measures by the drug industry. The manufacturers argue that price controls will hinder future innovations. On the other hand, a broad coalition of consumer associations and organizations of patients and senior citizens supports the current reform. They see the passing of the law as a major success and a step forward in their efforts. At the same time, Medi Cal recipients fear that they will lose access to drugs from manufacturers who do not comply with the price-reduction requirements.

Drug manufacturers want voluntary undertakings

It is expected that the average price reductions will be 40 percent on branded drugs and 60 percent on generics. Consumer representatives regard this law, which limits the enormous negotiating power of the drug manufacturers and pushes through lower prices, as a milestone. They also believe that the program will turn out to be the largest price-reduction action for prescription drugs in the United States to date. Because the drug companies have already spent $80 million to lobby against the reform, observers expect that they will make more efforts to prevent its implementation.

Expected price reduction: 40 percent on original products, 60 percent on generics

Sources and further reading:
Oppenheimer, Karen P. and Carol Medlin. "California Prescription Drug Discount Plan." *Health Policy Monitor*, October 2006. www.hpm.org/survey/us/c8/4.

"Prescription Discount Deal Reached. Drug firms not offering breaks to the uninsured would face sanctions." *The Sacramento Bee*, August 25, 2006. dwb.sacbee.com/content/politics/story/14307425p-15194046c.html.
"California Governor Signs Landmark Prescription Drug Discount Plan." *California Progress Report*, September 29, 2006. www.californiaprogressreport.com/2006/09/california_gove.html.
PhRMA. PhRMA Statement On CalRx Program. Press Release, September 29, 2006. www.phrma.org/news_room/press_releases/phrma_statement°n_calrx_program/.

United States: First experiences with health savings accounts

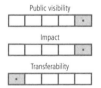

Public visibility

Impact

Transferability

Health savings accounts have mostly been associated with Singapore, which is working on ways for the chronically ill to use their savings more effectively—namely for ambulatory services (see page 66). But the reforms in the United States really have only the name in common with those in Singapore. The health savings accounts (HSAs) in the United States can only be properly understood in combination with the other side of the coin: high-deductible health plans (HDHPs). Both were introduced in 2003. Health savings accounts can be used to save money to pay for medical treatment when needed. Since the introduction of this reform, people on an insurance plan with a high deductible are able to open a health savings account. They must choose a deductible element of at least USD 1,000 and not more than $5,000 (about 770 to 3,850 euros), and for families $2,000 to $10,000. Insured people can pay an amount into their health savings account up to the level of the deductible. The money in the account is nontaxable and can be used to pay for medical services that the high-deductible health plan does not cover. Proponents of this model argue that insured people with HDHPs and HSAs would act more responsibly when it comes to their own health and would adopt a more healthful lifestyle (Trang Huynh 2004). In addition, the high-deductible plans in connection with savings accounts offer many Americans economical health insurance coverage tailored to meet their individual needs.

The positions adopted by the various social actors regarding high deductibles in combination with HSAs have remained more or less unchanged since they were introduced. Support for the model has come in particular from the president, the Republicans, health insurers and employers. They see high deductibles and savings accounts as a way of curbing healthcare costs by giving people more control over and responsibility for their health. Employers can reduce health insurance costs because the premiums for HDHPs are lower than for standard plans. Health insurers also profit from high-deductible plans. Savings as a result of the deduction of costs and co-payments exceed the losses due to the lower premiums.

High deductibles and savings accounts as a way to cut costs ...

Criticism of HDHPs and HSAs comes from the Democrats and organizations representing people without health insurance and low-income groups. They are worried that normal plans could become more expensive because healthy people will opt for the high-deductible plans. They also doubt whether patients will really be in a position to make informed decisions in favor of less expensive treatments. The majority of insured people have no access to adequate information about the costs and quality of medical benefits. The American Medical Association (AMA) is in favor of health savings accounts and has issued a positive statement. However, it seems that some doctors remain skeptical. They say that they cannot give their patients sound advice about how they should weigh costs and other factors that influence the decision for or against a type of treatment.

... but with risks

The number of insurers offering health savings accounts is growing—though from a low starting level. The proportion of employers offering their employees HSA products increased from 1 percent to 4 percent between 2004 and 2005. The Government Accountability Office estimates that 2 million to 3 million people have enrolled in health savings accounts. With 177 million people covered by private insurance (either through their employer or individually), this corresponds to only about 1.7 percent. However, the number has risen sharply since January 2005, when only about 600,000 people had such an account. Current estimates are that in 2010, 14 percent to 24 percent of all people enrolled in private insurance will have a health savings account.

The first studies indicate that the HDHP/HSA combination will lead to risk segmentation, a higher financial burden on people in poor health and an underuse of necessary health benefits. People with health savings accounts tend to have a disproportionately high income, and they are younger, healthier and better educated than people with standard health insurance. A survey by the Government Accountability Office, for example, came to the conclusion that state employees with a health savings account were twice as likely to have an income above USD 75,000 per year as employees without a health savings account. In addition, the study showed that holders of health savings accounts tended to delay or avoid necessary treatments more so than people with other insurance products. This effect is observable in particular among people who are in poor health and those with an income below USD 50,000.

Sources and further reading:
Poteliakhoff, Emmi. "Update on Health Savings Accounts (HSAs)." *Health Policy Monitor*, October 2006. www.hpm.org/survey/us/b8/4.
Trang Huynh, Phuong. "Health Savings Accounts (HSAs)." *Health Policy Monitor*, October 2004. www.hpm.org/survey/us/b4/1.

American Medical Association. Health Savings Accounts at a Glance. Chicago (Ill.), 2004. www.ama-assn.org/ama1/pub/upload/mm/363/hsabrochure.pdf.

American Medical Association. Policy Consolidation on Health System Reform. Report on the Council on Medical Services. CMS Report 7 – I-05, November 2005, p 8, Policy H-165.852. Health Savings Accounts. www.ama-assn.org/ama1/pub/upload/mm/372/i-05cmsreport7.pdf.

Carroll, John. HSAs. Early returns are in. *Managed Care Magazine* (14) 3, March 2005. www.managedcaremag.com/archives/0503/0503.HSAs.html.

Carroll, John. Banks give insurers an offer most of them cannot refuse. *Managed Care Magazine* (15) 7, July 2006. www.managedcaremag.com/archives/0607/0607.banks.html.

Claxton, Gary, Jon Gabel, Isadora Gil, Jeremy Pickreign, Heidi Whitmore, Benjamin Finder, Shada Rouhani, Samantha Hawkins and Diane Rowland. What High Deductible Plans Look Like. Findings From a National Survey of Employers. *Health Affairs* (24) 5 2005. 1273–1280.

Claxton, Gary, Jon Gabel, Isadora Gil, Jeremy Pickreign, Heidi Whitmore, Benjamin Finder, Bianca DiJulio and Samantha Hawkins. Health Benefits in 2006. Premium Increases Moderate, Enrollment In Consumer-Directed Health Plans Remains Modest. *Health Affairs* (25) 6 2006. w476–w485 (web exclusive, posting date: September 26, 2006).

Cross, Margaret Ann. Momentum Shifts Toward Consumer-Directed Plans. *Managed Care Magazine* (14) 7, July 2005. www.managedcaremag.com/archives/0507/0507.landscape.html.

Davis, Karen, Michelle M. Doty and Alice Ho. How High Is Too High? Implications of High-Deductible Health Plans. *Commonwealth Fund pub*. 816, April 2005. www.cmwf.org/usr_doc/816_Davis_how_high_is_too_high_impl_HDHPs.pdf.

Employee Benefit Research Institute, The Commonwealth Fund. Early Experience with High-Deductible and Consumer-Driven Health Plans. Findings from the EBRI/ Commonwealth Fund Consumerism in Health Care Survey. *Issue Brief* 288, December 2005. www.cmwf.org/usr_doc/fronstin_consumerism_survey.pdf.

Center on Budget and Policy Priorities. Expansion in HSA Tax Breaks is Larger—and More Problematic—than Previously Understood. Health Policy Analysis, February 4, 2006 (revised February 7, 2006). http://www.cbpp.org/2-4-06tax.htm.

United States Government Accountability Office. Consumer-Directed Health Plans. Small but growing enrollment fueled by rising cost of health care coverage. Report to the Chairman, Committee on the Budget, House of Representatives, April 2006. GAO-06-514. www.gao.gov/new.items/d06514.pdf.

United States Government Accountability Office. Federal Employees Health Benefits Program. Early experience with a consumer-directed health plan. Report to the Ranking Minority Member, Committee on Finance, U.S. Senate, November 2005. GAO-06-143. www.gao.gov/new.items/d06143.pdf.

Center on Budget and Policy Priorities. The Cost and Coverage Impact of the President's Health Insurance Budget Proposals. Health Policy Analysis, February 15, 2006. www.cbpp.org/2-15-06health.htm.

"Health Accounts Benefit Employers." *Wall Street Journal*, February 3, 2006.

Henry J. Kaiser Family Foundation, Health Research and Educational Trust. *Employer Health Benefits. Annual Survey 2005*. www.kff.org/insurance/7315/upload/7315.pdf.

Henry J. Kaiser Family Foundation, Health Research and Educational Trust. *Employer Health Benefits. 2006 Annual Survey*. www.kff.org/insurance/7527/upload/7527.pdf.

The White House, Office of Management and Budget. U.S. Analytical Perspectives, Budget of the United States Government, Fiscal Year 2007. Washington: U.S. Government Printing Office, 2006. www.whitehouse.gov/omb/budget/fy2007/pdf/spec.pdf.

Center on Budget and Policy Priorities. Administration Defense of Health Savings Accounts Rests on Misleading Use of Statistics. Health Policy Analysis, February 16, 2006. www.cbpp.org/2-16-06health.htm.

Remler, Dahlia, and Sherry Glied. How Much More Cost Sharing Will Health Savings Accounts Bring? *Health Affairs* (25) 4 2006. 1070–1078.

Alliance for Health Reform and Henry J. Kaiser Family Foundation. Where are HSAs and High-Deductible Health Plans Headed? Speech Transcript, March 10, 2006. www.kaisernetwork.org/health_cast/uploaded_files/031006_alliance_HSA_transcript.pdf.

United States: CMS publishes prices for hospital procedures

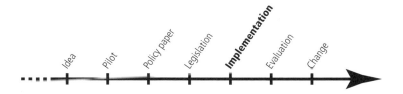

The Center for Medicare & Medicaid Services (CMS) is the U.S. federal agency that administers Medicare (the federal health insurance for people 65 and older and people with disabilities), Medicaid (the state health insurance program for the needy) and other state programs. Among its areas of responsibility are financing, benefits catalogues, and quality assurance.

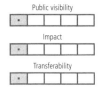

In June 2006, CMS published data on the Internet for the first time about hospital prices for 30 common procedures such as a hip replacement and cardiac surgery. The figures showed what Medicare paid for these procedures in a certain region. Data for individual hospitals is not provided. There are also no data available about what private insurance companies and patients paying

Price data published on the Internet

privately would have to pay for the same procedure. This is one of a series of measures aimed at introducing more transparency with respect to prices and quality in order to generate more competition between service providers and offer patients and insurance companies the possibility of making informed choices. But because the data are not related to individual hospitals, no observable impacts on demand behavior are expected.

Patient information to promote competition

A competitive health system is a central concern of the administration of George W. Bush. It promotes the individual responsibility of patients and offers them increased freedom of choice. The government encourages hospitals and doctors to publish the prices of their services and is considering whether this should be compelled by law. The publication of prices by CMS is seen as a step toward giving people more information so that they can base their choice of medical benefits on the price and quality of the service offered.

CMS price data will not have much effect

It is not likely that the CMS's publication of price data at the regional level will lead to an intensification of competition or changes in patients' behavior. Patients cannot compare individual hospitals directly with one another. In addition, there is no information about the quality of care in each hospital. But this would be important for an informed choice because it can be assumed that patients will not make a choice of hospital solely on the basis of price.

Sources and further reading:
Poteliakhoff, Emmi. "Price data published by CMS: 'Payer Power Plan.'" *Health Policy Monitor*, October 2006. www. hpm.org/survey/us/b8/3.

"Medicare posts 30 procedures' prices." *USA Today*, June 2, 2006.
The White House. President Discusses Health Care Initiatives. Press Release, May 1, 2006. www.whitehouse.gov/ news/releases/2006/05/20060501-5.html.
Centers for Medicare and Medicaid Services. *Fact Sheet. Helping Patients Get the Best Care For Their Needs*, June 1, 2006.

Centers for Medicare and Medicaid Services. Medicare Posts Hospital Payment Information. Press release, June 1, 2006. www.hhs.gov/news/press/2006pres/20060601a.html.

Henry J. Kaiser Family Foundation. Minnesota Health Insurers Post Price Data Online to Meet Consumer Demand. Daily Health Policy Report, November 9, 2005. www.kaisernetwork.org/daily_reports/rep_hpolicy_recent_rep.cfm?dr_cat=3&show=yes&dr_DateTime=11-09-05#33621.

"CQ HealthBeat Examines Bush Administration Plan to Improve Price Transparency; HealthGrades Offers Price Reports for a Fee." *Medical News Today*, March 22, 2006. www.medicalnewstoday.com/medicalnews.php?newsid=39928.

Community Oncology Alliance. Medicare to Post Price Data on June 1 under Transparency Plan. News article, May 2, 2006. www.communityoncology.org/Default.aspx?tabid=82&ctl=Details&mid=404&ItemID=570.

Health and long-term care insurance

Efforts to provide an equitably financed healthcare system that provides as many services as possible for the entire population are central in debates about health policy. Despite constraints on government spending, many industrialized countries are extending their collectively funded health systems in order to improve access for the entire population to more effective services of a higher quality. In addition to broadening the system and including groups not previously covered, the rationalization of health services also plays an increasingly important role in dealing with growing cost pressures. Fig. 2 shows the three dimensions of health policy decisions that influence the effectiveness and financial viability of health systems. They can be viewed as the breadth, depth and height of publicly financed services. *Breadth* in this context is defined as the extent of the population covered by the service; *depth* is the scope of the catalogue of services; *height* is the proportion of total costs for those services that are publicly funded. The theoretical effort to fill out the box as much as possible is encapsulated in the founding motto from 1948 of the British NHS: "universal, comprehensive, and free at the point of use."

With the exception of the United States, almost all industrialized countries have a universal health insurance system that covers all or almost all of the population. Such systems display a considerable level of solidarity because the healthy and the sick, young and old, rich and poor, men and women, families and individuals bear the costs for the (basic) care together, and generally speaking the strong provide financial support for the weak.

Universal insurance coverage predominant

Historically, universal coverage has been achieved sooner in countries with tax-funded health systems than in contribution-funded systems. The Scandinavian countries and New Zealand

95

Fig. 2: The three dimensions of decisions about the financing of services

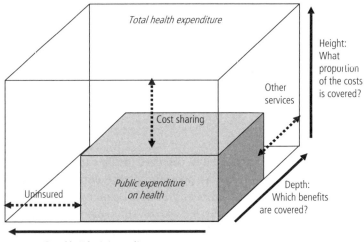

Source: Expanded from Busse, Schreyögg and Gericke 2007

were already reaching the goal of universal coverage in the 1930s and 1940s; the development in countries with social health insurance (SHI) models took longer, and they began to reach universal coverage in the 1990s. One of the reasons for this is that in social health insurance systems, only those individuals paying contributions are directly covered. As the economy grew, people who did not have employment through which they made social insurance contributions were also gradually included—first members of the family, then pensioners and the unemployed, students, and finally the self-employed. Switzerland (1996), France (2000) and the Netherlands (2006) are the best examples of social health insurance systems that have introduced legislation on universal health insurance coverage only in the past 10 years. In countries that have private health insurance as an alternative alongside the social insurance or tax-funded system (for higher earners and the self-employed, for example), compensation mechanisms must be developed so that the publicly funded system is supported by the economic strength of the entire population. In the Netherlands, this was the case until 2005, that is, as long as a dual insurance system existed, with a surcharge on premiums for private health insurance going to the central SHI fund, and secondly with tax revenues that were also channeled into the central fund for the statutory health insurance system (cf. pages 25–26).

In the United States, where the only health and long-term care insurance based on collective funding is the Medicare program for the elderly, individual states have repeatedly tried to introduce a universal health insurance system. Massachusetts is implementing a law on universal health insurance that was approved in April 2006 (see page 100). This demonstrates the political will to ensure full coverage for the entire population. Another example of such a political initiative is in Spain, where the government has introduced a fourth pillar in the social-insurance system in the form of national insurance for long-term care for the entire population (see page 102).

Apart from the question of what part of the population is insured, the depth of the benefit basket also plays a key role when it comes to the public funding of a health system. Although the topic of benefit baskets arouses considerable interest, not much is really understood about the different sorts of baskets. This is, first, because the decision-making procedures for inclusion and reimbursement of new treatments or drugs into benefit baskets vary considerably between countries—from an explicit list of all funded services as an annex to the Health Insurance Act in Israel to a vaguely formulated provision in Britain that the health minister has to include and reimburse services that he deems necessary "within reasonable limits" (NHS charter). Second, there is no international classification of health benefits that would allow a comparison in detail. For a long time it was claimed that tax-funded systems often had no detailed basket of benefits, whereas the majority of statutory health insurance systems necessarily did—first because of the defined benefits to which the insured are entitled and second because of the need to remunerate providers for the services they provide. The EU-funded Health BASKET project has shown that this view of things is oversimplified. For example, Italy and Spain, which are tax-funded systems, have in part very detailed lists of benefits, whereas in the German hospital sector only a very short negative list exists (Schreyögg et al. 2005).

Despite (or perhaps because of) the absence of a detailed list of benefits, Great Britain has become a trailblazer in the creation

Range of services not internationally uniform

of evaluation institutions with its National Institute for Health and Clinical Excellence (NICE). Its charge is to make recommendations for the inclusion or exclusion of drugs and technologies in the benefit basket on the basis of their efficiency and cost effectiveness—and for the conditions under which benefits should be provided (cf. report on page 54).

In addition to the trend to include more services in the benefit basket, diametrically opposite developments can also be observed: Dentistry and aids such as glasses or walking aids are being explicitly removed from the benefit basket in some countries, among them Germany, whereas countries such as Spain and Great Britain are introducing, reintroducing or retaining those benefits. A recent example of changes in the benefit basket comes from Singapore, where funding will be available for selected disease management programs carried out on an outpatient basis (see page 109).

Payments intended to promote cost awareness Private contributions to healthcare costs by some form of cost-sharing for outpatient and inpatient treatments have developed in very different ways in recent years in industrialized countries. In about half of the EU member states, cost sharing is required for primary and secondary care. A co-payment or a percentage of the costs is charged for prescription drugs in all countries except the Netherlands, where each group of drugs includes at least one product whose price lies below the maximum remuneration level (reference price) and is available without co-payment. With the Act to Improve Efficiency in Pharmaceutical Care, which came into force in Germany in July 2006, drugs whose prices are at least 30 percent below the reference price are free from co-payment.

According to OECD figures, private expenditures on drugs in 2003 accounted for 25.2 percent of total expenditure on drugs in Germany, 32.8 percent in France and 42.6 percent in the Netherlands. In many industrialized countries, politicians justify increased payments as the only way to avoid exploitation of the system ("moral hazard") and thus to preserve solidarity in funding.

Compensation for the socially disadvantaged The socially disadvantaged and the elderly are disproportionately affected by increasing private payments, and without compensation mechanisms there would be a reduction in the level of financial solidarity. In many countries, supplementary insurance

98

is offered that covers the cost sharing payments. Most people are able to afford supplementary insurance, but a section of the population has no access to this type of insurance because of financial reasons, health reasons, or both. Some countries have recognized these problems and are trying to fill the coverage gaps through additional legislation. For example, the socially disadvantaged in France may buy private insurance using publicly subsidized health insurance credits (see page 105). In Slovenia, risk structure compensation was introduced to prevent private health insurers from selecting only low-risk customers ("cream skimming") and thus to prevent the exclusion of the sick and the elderly (see page 107).

In the future, cost increases resulting from further innovations and an aging population will exert constant pressure on the funding of health systems in industrialized countries. Collectively funded health systems can withstand this pressure if they apply rational evaluation methods for the inclusion of treatments in the benefit catalogue and increase patients' awareness about expenditures for health benefits while taking social inequalities into consideration.

Demographic developments make rationalization necessary

Sources and further reading:

Busse, Reinhard, and Annette Riesberg. *Health Care Systems in Transition – Germany.* Copenhagen: WHO Regional Office for Europe on behalf of the European Observatory on Health Systems and Policies, 2004.

Busse, Reinhard, Jörg Schreyögg and Christian Gericke. *Analyzing Changes in Health Financing Arrangements in High Income Countries.* HNP Discussion Paper. Washington DC: World Bank, 2007.

Henke, Klaus-Dirk, and Jonas Schreyögg. *Towards sustainable health care systems:* Strategies in health insurance schemes in France, Germany, Japan and the Netherlands. (Sec.Ed.). Berlin: International Social Security Association, 2005.

OECD. *Health at a Glance. OECD Indicators 2005.* Paris: OECD, 2005.

Schreyögg, Jonas, Tom Stargardt, Marcial Velasco-Garrido and Reinhard Busse. Defining the benefit basket in nine European countries. Evidence from the EU Health BASKET project. *The European Journal of Health Economics* (6) Supplement: 2–10, 2005.

Saltman, Richard B., Reinhard Busse and Josep Figueras. *Social health insurance systems in Western Europe.* Berkshire: Open University Press, 2004.

United States: Massachusetts—health insurance for all

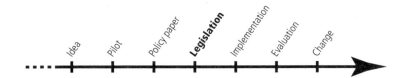

Public visibility

Impact

Transferability

In April 2006 the Massachusetts legislature voted by an overwhelming majority for a new health insurance bill. The law coming into effect in July 2007 provides for collective health insurance coverage on the basis of the existing system of private health insurance. The aim of the government is to have 99 percent of the population with insurance coverage by 2010. Various incentive systems will be used to include the 515,000 people—approximately 8 percent of the population—who have been without insurance.

Lower premiums through collective insurance

The bill envisages the inclusion of all 19- to 26-year-olds. This age group currently has hardly any health insurance coverage because of the high costs coupled with a relatively low perceived risk. With this obligation, the government is trying to increase the level of solidarity in health insurance. Young people tend to pay more than they reclaim in the form of benefits and thus they strengthen the revenue side. Higher overall revenues can in turn lead to more favorable average premiums.

Penalties for breaches

The obligation to take out health insurance will be enforced through the introduction of financial incentives and penalties for

100

both employees and employers. The state will offer tax waivers on insurance agreements for companies with fewer than 50 employees as an incentive for firms to take out health insurance for their staff. It is expected that about 215,000 previously uninsured will be newly covered by health insurance through this measure.

The bill requires insurers to ensure a monthly insurance premium of around USD 200. Low earners are offered less expensive packages from the private health insurers, although with a restricted range of benefits. For those with incomes at or below 300 percent of the poverty level (about 22,400 euros per person), the government of Massachusetts provides financial support with the cost for health insurance. Children from poor families receive free access to health care through Medicaid. These measures are intended to lead to a more equitable insurance system because everybody from the richest to the poorest is taking part. A newly created institution will implement the law and supervise its progress.

Special conditions for the working poor

One reason for the rapid formulation of the bill was pressure from the federal government. Because of the high proportion of people who were without health insurance in Massachusetts, the state had been threatened with a cut of USD 385 million from the national Medicaid fund.

After months of discussions about the level of penalties for employers who fail to insure employees—a fine of up to USD 800 was proposed but the idea was dropped completely in the end, after a line-item veto by the governor—the bill introduced by Sen. Romney finally received broad support. It offers advantages for the population, private insurers and providers. Massachusetts is the first U.S. state to legislate for general health insurance coverage for its population, following failed initiatives in Hawaii (see report in *Health Policy Developments,* issue 1), Minnesota and Vermont.

Broad agreement from all sides

The government of Massachusetts expects additional costs of USD 1.2 billion in the next three years as a result of the new law, although only USD 125 million will be drawn from the state budget. The rest will be covered by existing state resources and national funds. It is expected that after 2010, no new state funds will be needed to finance the new health insurance system. It remains to be seen whether the new law will fulfill the high hopes placed on it, and the federal government now has to decide whether it will really cut the USD 385 million from the national Medicaid fund—a decision that will be critical to the success or failure of the new insurance initiative.

Sources and further reading:
Schulz, Anke Therese and Carol Medlin. "Massachusetts Health Coverage Mandate." *Health Policy Monitor*, April 6, 2006. www.hpm.org/survey/us/c7/3.

Massachusetts Government. Implementation of Health Care Law Proceeds. www.mass.gov/?pageID=press-releases&agId=Agov2&prModName=gov2press-release&prFile=gov_pr_060501_healthcare_waiver.xml.

Spain: National insurance for long-term care

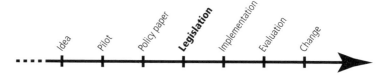

The Spanish Ministry of Labor and Social Affairs has drafted a law for insurance for long-term care that will be introduced between 2007 and 2015 as a fourth pillar of the social security system. The objective is to make care available more efficiently and in a way better suited to people's needs. The law envisages three types of support. First, it would increase the personal freedom of those in need of care by providing extended outpatient care and funding alterations to living space. Second, it would promote the integration of outpatient and inpatient care by establishing new institutions and also improving the training of nursing staff. Third, relatives could apply for financial support for the long-term care they provide. This would be dependent on the financial situation of the person receiving care and the degree of care needed.

The new long-term care insurance act applies to the entire population and will be funded in equal parts by the national government, the autonomous regions, and the persons needing care. The regions must transfer their annual share, 3.5 billion euros, to the national government. But they will continue to be responsible for the provision of care institutions. Funding for long-term care will be ensured by the savings that will be gained in the health system in the regions, because the costs for many chronically ill patients will no longer be met through the health system but through the long-term care insurance. A patient treated in a stationary setting costs the health system on average 360 euros per day, in contrast to expected costs of only 60 euros per day per patient with the new approach and the long-term care insurance.

Law eases financial burden on health system

The draft bill to improve care of the old and the disabled has been discussed in Spain for more than a decade. According to a survey in 1999, more than 1.5 million Spaniards are in need of assistance or long-term care. Two-thirds of them are 65 or older. The current access to care benefits is very restricted, and 65 percent of those needing long-term care have no access to care institutions. In these cases, relatives or partners provide unpaid care for an average of 10 hours daily.

Inadequate care for long-term care patients in the past

The Toledo Agreement in 2003 was the first step toward establishing long-term care insurance at the national level. The core of the agreement consisted of proposals to reform social security in old age (see report in *Health Policy Developments*, issue 2). The problem encountered at that time was reaching a consensus between the national government and the 17 autonomous regions, which have far-reaching powers relating to the health care of their populations.

Decentralization makes national consensus more difficult

As a precursor to the current act, a program was introduced in the province Castile and Leon in 2003 for the improved integration of medical and social services. Coordination teams were set up there with the task of creating an integrated system to look after those in need of long-term care (see report in issue 2).

The law proposes a national council for long-term care insurance to coordinate the regional bodies while taking government decisions into account. In addition, two advisory bodies will be set up, consisting of representatives of the government, employers' and employees' associations, and representatives of the old and

Coordination at national level

infirm. By including important representatives in the coordination, the ministry has obtained broad support for the legislation.

The regions are supporting a national plan because according to a report of the Spanish Society for Geriatrics and Gerontology, the number of people more than 80 years old—the high-risk group—has risen to 8.8 percent of the population. The increase shows slight regional variations, as does the distribution of existing care institutions.

Despite the agreement reached, many of the associations still fear that the homogeneity anticipated with national long-term care insurance will not be achieved. Moral hazard and growing access barriers for many of those in need of long-term care as a result of the high co-payments could lead to considerable imbalances. The associations are therefore demanding a second step that would include the long-term care insurance in the tax-financed social security system, so that funding is ensured. A further problem is the wide variations in the distribution of geriatric institutions. Areas with a large percentage of elderly people have relatively fewer geriatric beds available than areas with lower proportions of old people. This will be one of the problems that the national system will have to address. The first evaluation is planned for 2012.

Sources and further reading:
Sánchez, Elvira, and Esther Martinez. "Integrated care for the elderly." Health Policy Monitor, April 2006. www.hpm.org/survey/es/a7/1.

Ministerio de Trabajo y asuntos sociales (2004). Atención a las personas en situación de dependencia en España. Libro Blanco. www.infodisclm.com/Dossieres/dependencia/libro_blanco_dependencia.pdf [in Spanish].
Ministerio de Trabajo y asuntos sociales (2006). Declaración. Para la promoción de la vida autónoma y dencia. www.tt.mtas.es [in Spanish].
Seminario de intervención y políticas sociales (2006). Informe sobre el anteproyecto de ley de promoción de la

France: Health insurance credits for the needy— only modest success

While Compulsory Health Insurance covers all of the population in France, co-payments by patients can be quite significant, especially for certain types of care where they can reach an average of 30 percent. To meet the high co-payments, about 85 percent of the population have private supplementary insurance (mutuelle) and about 7 percent (the poorest of the population) benefit from a publicly funded supplementary coverage (Couverture Maladie Universelle Complémentaire or CMUC). The rest (about 30 percent of the low income group) who are not poor enough to be eligible for CMUC are covered only by basic compulsory insurance. Therefore, since 2005 people with an annual income that does not exceed the poverty limit of 8,100 euros by more than 15 percent have been legally entitled to health insurance credits for supplementary health insurance.

The French government has introduced the credit voucher system as a way to redress an imbalance in health insurance within the population (see *Health Policy Developments*, issue 4). People with average or high incomes are able to afford additional insurance coverage without any real problems, and people whose income lies below the poverty line (7,045 euro per year) are exempt from co-payments, receiving CMUC. The law is aimed at the group of low earners who find themselves without any supplementary health insurance coverage.

Credits for low earners

Evaluation shows
moderate response

In its first annual evaluation, the national health insurance fund investigated the prices and the coverage offered by the new insurance credit voucher system. Of the 402,000 people entitled to apply for credits, 220,000 have done so in the first year. Of these, only 178,335 have actually used their credit vouchers. It is noticeable that only 14 percent of persons 60 and older used a credit voucher, whereas the figure for all other age groups was about 40 percent.

Credit vouchers
cover only part
of the costs

The reason for the moderate response could be the annual cost of the supplementary insurance premiums. In 2005, the cost was 430 euros on average. By contrast, the value of the credit vouchers was between 75 and 250 euros, depending on age and household situation. The big gap between the value of the vouchers and the actual costs of a supplementary insurance seems to be the reason why so many credit vouchers have not been used. Since January 2006, the difference was reduced considerably by an average increase in the value of a credit voucher of 33 percent; for persons 60 and older, the increase was about 60 percent. The maximum sum in this group then increased from 250 to about 400 euros. The ministry expects a considerable increase in the prevalence of voluntary extra insurance among elderly low earners.

Lack of
transparency

Nevertheless, many of the people supposed to benefit from the measure still feel that they have no access to it. The official term used in the law is a tax credit (credit d'impôt), and since many of those who would be entitled do not pay any income tax, they do not feel that the law applies to them.

Credit vouchers
as an effective
strategy?

The goal of the law is a positive one, because it leads to more equitable conditions for access to heath care. Nevertheless, many scientists are questioning whether health insurance credits and the bureaucracy and legal complications they involve are an efficient way to ensure broad access to the benefits of the health system. So far only about 45 percent of the target population has profited from the credit vouchers.

Experts are also asking whether the credit system will lead to moral hazards. Insurers could profit from the credit voucher system by increasing the prices but not the extent of the benefits provided. For their part, the people using the credit vouchers might draw on health benefits that they do not really need. These things are being looked at in the first evaluation.

Sources and further reading:

Franc, Carine, and Marc Perronnin. "Health insurance voucher plan: mid-term evaluation." *Health Policy Monitor.* April 2006. www.hpm.org/survey/fr/a7/3.

Auvray, Laurence, Anne Doussin, and Philippe Le Fur. "Santé, soins et protection sociale en 2002". Enquête sur la santé et la protection sociale (ESPS) France. 2002. Rapport n° 1509. 2003 [in French].

Fonds de financement de la protection complémentaire de la couvrture universelle du risque maladie. "Crédit d'impot". http://www.fonds-cmu.fr/site/index.php4?PHPSESSID=7867b4a5ef55b772c3bf252ff66118bb [in French].

Slovenia: Risk-structure compensation for supplementary insurance

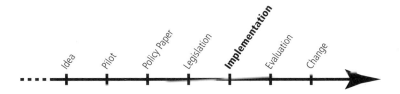

After years of cream skimming by private supplementary insurers, the Slovenian government in January 2006 introduced a risk-structure compensation law. This was urgently needed because the three established health insurance companies had tried by means of varying premium offers to discourage high-risk applicants. At the same time, the new law tries to introduce variation into the market for supplementary insurance. Insurance packages can now be offered that go farther than just providing coverage for additional payments for medical services. In the past, the supplementary insurance only covered all private co-payments, which account for 5 percent to 75 percent of medical benefits.

Following the 13.5 percent increase in premiums for persons over 60 by Vzajemna, the largest and oldest private supplemen-

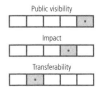

Long debate about cream skimming

107

tary insurer, there have been discussions in Slovenia about how to prevent cream skimming by these companies. The insurers maintained that the Vzajemna client structure was worse than that of the other two insurers, because they had extreme price differences and therefore were only attractive to young people.

In view of the fact that 94 percent of all those with statutory health insurance also have supplementary insurance coverage, many politicians suggested that the costs should be paid entirely through the statutory health insurance scheme. They argued that this method would be fairer, particularly for low earners, who could not afford the expensive supplementary insurance. Another argument in favor of this proposal was that it would help the national health insurance institute improve the negative financial results in recent years, because the supplementary insurers generated good profits over the same period. After the presidential elections in 2004, the new conservative government decided to keep the supplementary insurance, but with legal changes for the insurers.

Compensation between insurers The health insurance companies are now required to accept all people with statutory health insurance, and all must offer the same premium. A rebate of up to 3 percent is allowed if the insurance can demonstrate that administrative costs are very low. The insurers are not allowed to terminate contracts as long as the clients pay their premiums regularly. The health ministry supervises compliance with the law and calculates possible compensation payments between the insurers. These are based on the average age and the sexual distribution of the customers of each insurer.

Customers show high mobility With the introduction of the law, people now have the option of changing their insurance without loss, and about 25 percent of customers have made use of this option. Vzajemna suffered considerable losses, because many people changed to one of the other two smaller companies. These offer a wider range of insurance coverage beyond the payments for medical treatment, and they have promised higher quality standards. The two health insurers belong to two large general insurance groups, so that they are also expected to offer their customers services in addition to health insurance.

Older people pay less Overall, the introduction of the risk structure compensation has led to a fairer distribution of costs for supplementary insurance to cover private co-payments. While older people now pay a lower premium, there has not been a change in the average insurance premium. The quality improvements promised by the two smaller insurance companies have not yet been realized, and it is doubtful whether they will be in the future. This will require more far-reaching reforms in the field of health insurance.

Sources and further reading:
Albreht, Tit. "Risk equalising schemes for voluntary insurance." *Health Policy Monitor*, November 2005. www.hpm.org/survey/si/a6/2.

Doenoviè Bonèa, Petra, and Maks Tajnikar. Recent developments in the voluntary health insurance market in Slovenia, 2005. www.ef.uni-lj.si/konferenca/gradiva/Dosenovic_Tajnikar.pdf.

Singapore: New financing for outpatient disease management programs

For the first time in Singapore, outpatient treatment will be financed through the statutory medical savings account scheme (Medisave). In 2007, patients with the four most common chronic conditions (diabetes mellitus, hypertension, strokes, and lipid disorders) will be able to take part in outpatient disease management programs (DMP).

In the past, about 1 million patients with the four chronic diseases had to be treated in hospital in order to qualify for Medisave funding. The result was overfilled hospitals and intermittent

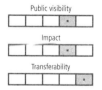

Improved quality of care

109

treatment of the chronically ill. The health ministry expects that the disease management programs will offer better results because it will be possible to treat chronically ill patients more regularly and in a more standardized fashion. Regular communication between hospitals and general practitioners will also lead to a smooth transition of care for the four patient groups. The ministry assumes that in the long term there will be considerable savings in comparison with the former expensive inpatient treatments.

General practitioners as DMP coordinators

General practitioners, who in the past have had a very much limited sphere of responsibility, will be able to register for the four disease management programs. After registration, they will receive further training that will enable them to treat patients on the basis of evidence-based protocols. The Health Ministry has commissioned experts to draw up the protocols on the basis of international standards.

Annual budget for the chronically ill

The program will be financed by individual budgets. Withdrawals will be subject to an annual limit of SGD 300 per Medisave account. Second, a co-payment of 15 percent will be set on each outpatient bill in excess of a deductible of SGD 30. Bills below SGD 30 will continue to be paid in cash. In order to monitor the quality of the care provided, Medisave will be carrying out surveys of the doctors involved. In all, the ministry estimates that 1 million patients could be included in one of the four programs.

Approval for introduction of the outpatient programs

Both patients and doctors approve of the new development because the current inpatient treatment of the chronically ill is not ideal. Patients at home after or between treatments seem to take medication irregularly or do not request new drugs when needed in order to avoid the expense.

The government supports the idea of the outpatient program because it is repeatedly facing problems with hospitals that are filled to overflowing. At the same time, though, many politicians are worried that the new program will involve extra expenditure and possible moral hazard, so that the financing of Medisave could be threatened. This is why the implementation of the plans includes an annual limit and co-payments, in order to avoid health shopping. Patients advocates remain critical of the high co-payments which could be an insurmountable barrier to participation for many patients. Non-participating general practitioners complain that it could lead to the development of two classes of family doctors.

It remains to be seen how successful the idea of outpatient treatment for patients with the four most common conditions will be in the disease management program.

Sources and further reading:

Lim, Meng Kin. "Liberalization of Medisave Use." *Health Policy Monitor*, April 2006. www.hpm.org/survey/sg/a7/2.

Ministry of Health. Better Health Outcomes for the Chronically-Ill Through Structured Disease Management Programmes. www.moh.gov.sg/corp/about/newsroom/press releases/details.do ?id=36962319.

Patient orientation

Patient orientation and communication—the active integration of patients or insured individuals in health system processes—plays a key role in current reforms aimed at improving the quality of care. In most health systems, demand continues to be shaped by supply, that is, the treatments offered by the providers of health care. This observation is neither new nor surprising. The situation is the result of natural information asymmetries between providers and users of health services. The inadequate explanation of treatment options by doctors further reinforces the dependence of the patients. Health policies are also frequently formulated without giving due consideration to the needs of the patients, especially if they do not have a well-organized lobby. Patients often regard the health system as obscure and difficult to understand. Many have not been informed about the objectives of their own therapy. Information from the Internet can increase the confusion rather than bring clarification.

Improving the orientation to the needs of the patient can lower the barriers to communication and understanding. Patients as individuals should be put in a position to inquire about the treatment adopted by the doctor, with decisions being reached jointly. Patients as a group should contribute to the improvement of structures and processes.

In the past, processes and the results of treatment in the health system were not transparent for patients. It was not possible to make choices on the basis of quality indicators. With the publication of evaluations, some countries are endeavoring to make hospitals and other health institutions comparable for patients. The French health ministry has developed benchmarks for the incidence of hospital infections. This means that hospitals

Make comparative quality transparent

have an additional incentive to take more effective steps to avoid infections. In 2008, the data will be made public so that patients will be able to compare hospitals (see page 115). In Finland, since 2006 the annual statistical report has included benchmark indicators for the efficiency of hospitals in the treatment of specific diseases. Patients can compare the country's hospitals on the basis of these parameters (see page 118).

In Germany, hospitals are required to document their quality for the treatment of a series of diseases. The processes and outcomes are evaluated by the Federal Office for Quality Assurance (*BQS*). Because all hospitals are required to take part in this external quality assurance, the results are of international significance. However, so far only aggregate datasets have been published, so that it is not possible to identify the quality of individual hospitals. Media reports about clinics in the Rhine-Ruhr district and in Berlin that included data about specific hospitals are the first steps toward change. A second weakness of German activity in this area is that it has so far concentrated almost exclusively on surgical indications.

Simplify access for patients In addition to the opportunities for comparison of institutions, a key factor is giving patients access to health care. Investigations show that lack of access—whether for financial, organizational, or other reasons—is perceived by many patients as their greatest problem (see *Health Policy Developments*, issue 4, as well as chapter on Access in this volume). A focus on primary care is intended to offer patients easier access to the health system.

Including the public in health questions In order to improve primary health care in England and Wales, the health ministry commissioned a survey to determine priorities and previous problems that it could address in its new strategy (see page 120). Estonia has involved the population in preparing for reform of primary care with a written questionnaire. On the basis of the responses, Estonia set up a doctors' hotline in August 2005 that is available 24 hours a day (see page 122).

Information campaigns generate transparency Raising public awareness about possibilities for involvement can increase transparency and the autonomy of patients. For example, in Israel the finance ministry (together with the auditing office) has published a brochure explaining the advantages and disadvantages of insurance for long-term care and the various offers.

114

The multilingual brochure was included as a supplement in a free weekend newspaper to reach the entire population quickly (see page 124).

Dissemination through the mass media

A government can introduce legislation to strengthen the rights of individuals to be involved in their own health care. An example of this is a new law in Austria. Since March 2006, patients have been empowered to draw up a living will, specifying the treatment they wish to receive in the event that they are unable to give informed consent (see page 126).

Living will of the patient instead of duties of caregivers

> *Sources and further reading:*
> Busse, Reinhard, and Annette Riesberg. *Health Care Systems in Transition – Germany*. Copenhagen: WHO Regional Office for Europe on behalf of the European Observatory on Health Systems and Policies, 2004.

France: Quality benchmarks to reduce infections in hospitals

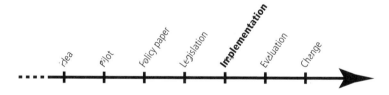

Estimates suggest that 7 percent of patients admitted to hospitals in France every year become infected during their stay. In February 2006, an official ranking list was presented for the first time that compares how hospitals are combating the spread of infections within their walls.

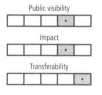

Infections caused by hospital germs cost the health service about 200 million euros a year. The quality benchmark is intended to induce hospitals to invest more in the prevention of infections and thus to improve the quality of the care they provide, while also lowering costs.

More transparency…

The first published benchmark index, ICALIN (L'Indicateur Composite des Activités de Lutte contre les Infections Nosoco-

…as an incentive to act

miales), consists of about 30 items and has three dimensions: finances, organizational structures and activities to counter hospital infections. Further indicators to be published include the consumption of antiseptic hand wash per 1,000 hospital days, the incidence of *Staphylococcus aureus* (a very resistant germ), the incidence of infections as side effects of surgical interventions, and the consumption of antibiotics. The infection rates for each hospital will not be made public.

On the basis of the indicators, a hospital is graded from A (very good) to E (very poor). The average grade is determined for all the hospitals in a class. There are 13 classes of hospitals, varying in the number of beds, the type of care and private or public status.

Public pressure forces action

Tackling infections in hospitals has been on the list of priorities since 1998 for the National Health Conference, at which medical specialist associations, health insurers and the health ministry are represented. In 1999, some journalists produced *Le guide des hôspitaux*, which compares mortality rates in hospitals on the basis of numbers of various cases. Despite energetic protests from the hospitals about the methods used to gather the data, the public response to the book was very positive, and the health ministry was forced to develop and implement a more solid framework to measure the performance of individual hospitals. In 2000, the ministry issued a decree for the coordination of specific actions to reduce infections in hospitals.

Local, regional and national approach

All hospitals must set up a committee to draw up an annual action plan to reduce infections. At the regional level, five infection centers (CCLIN) have been established to coordinate and supervise the collection of data by hospitals. At the national level, the ministry has set up a technical committee (CTIN) to identify focus topics and to assist with technical problems. Over the past six years, these measures have cost 78 million euros and created about 700 jobs.

Participation so far voluntary

After relevant indicators had been developed by health experts, pilot benchmarking began in 2003. Between 2003 and 2006, 40 hospitals took part in the project on a voluntary basis, during which 25 of the original 30 indicators were selected for data registration.

Ambitious goals for 2008

The objective of the health ministry is to generate indicator-specific datasets for all hospitals. Thirteen percent of hospitals have still not submitted figures. Another goal for 2008 is to reduce the incidence rate of staphylococcus by 25 percent in at least 75 percent of all hospitals. From 2008 onward, there should be no more hospitals in class E. The ministry expects that the targets will lead to hospitals increasing their consumption of antiseptic hand wash lotion by 75 percent.

Infection rates for specific organizations have not yet been made public. According to a public survey, 63 percent of those questioned believe that the incidence of infections in hospitals has continued to increase between 2004 and 2006, although in fact the incidence in public hospitals has declined for the first time. This difference in perception has to do with the influence of the media on public opinion. But in 2008, public opinions about infection rates might change. Then, according to the health ministry, clear figures will show the success of the fight against infections in hospitals.

Public still skeptical

Sources and further reading:
Or, Zeynep. "Benchmarking quality to fight hospital infections." *Health Policy Monitor*, April 2006. www.hpm.org/survey/fr/a7/2.

Ministère de la santé et des solidarités. "Décret no 99-1034 du 6 décembre 1999 relatif à l'organisation de la lutte contre les infections nosocomiales dans les établissements de santé et modifiant le chapitre Ier du titre Ier du livre VII du code de la santé publique (deuxième partie: Décrets en Conseil d'Etat)". www.legifrance.gouv.fr/WAspad/UnTexteDeJorf? numjo=MESH9923097D. Paris 1999 [in French].

Ministère de la santé et des solidarités. "Le tableau de bord des infectiosn nosocomiales. Indicatreur composite des achtivités de lutte conre les infections nosocomiales 2004 (ICALIN)". www.sante.gouv.fr/icalin/accueil.htm. Paris 2006 [in French].

Finland: Hospital evaluation for increased cost-effectiveness

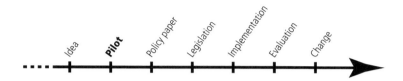

Public visibility

Impact

Transferability

In 2006, Finland began to include benchmark data from hospital evaluations in the national statistical database. In addition to routine data, effect parameters were determined for specific diseases on the basis of which the inefficiencies of previous processes could be identified. Pilot projects are currently evaluating the effectiveness of individual hospitals and hospital regions in the treatment of cardiac infarcts, hip fractures, schizophrenia, strokes, breast cancer, and hip prostheses. The aim of the evaluations is to increase the quality of treatment. To begin with, the benchmarks concentrated on large, economically relevant groups of patients, where restructuring and improved processes could lead to large savings.

DRGs as standard indicators

Since 1997, benchmark tests have been used for the treatment of inpatients and outpatients in order to determine relevant parameters and hence the productivity of hospitals. Ninety-five percent of Finnish hospitals have taken part in the benchmark testing, which is carried out in cooperation with the National Research and Development Centre for Welfare and Health (STAKES) and the hospital districts. In contrast to earlier measurements that were based on admission data, diagnosis related groups (DRGs) were used for the standardized determination of patient groups. Data sets are taken annually from the patient data systems of the hospitals.

Analysis possible at various levels

In addition to the productivity for individual DRG groups, it is also possible to evaluate and compare special fields and individual departments. The use of universal codes in all regions of Finland makes it possible to compare the average provision of care and treatment in Finnish hospitals. The deviations from the mean due to inefficiencies can be determined as well as the use of health services by any individual. With the help of the benchmark data, hospitals and hospital regions can draw up plans to improve efficiency and can exchange experience with other hospitals and regions.

A key question is the reliability of the data from the hospital information systems. However, experts assume that the good networking of patient data systems within the hospitals will provide consistent data. The necessary data sets can be accessed for analysis from a central point in the hospital.

Benchmarking in hospitals has considerable potential for the future. Comprehensive information that is always up to date can provide hospital managers with a basis for cost reductions and improvements in quality. Using the data for specific effect parameters, Finnish hospitals expect to be able to carry out changes in strategies and operational procedures.

Great potential for the future

Sources and further reading:
Linna, Miika. "Benchmarking hospital productivity." *Health Policy Monitor,* April 2006. www.hpm.org/survey/fi/a7/4.

Linna, Miika. Benchmarking in Finnish hospitals. Towards more efficient care. National Research and Development Centre for Welfare and Health. norddrg.kuntaliitto.fi/linna.htm.

Linna, Miika, Jutta Niemel, Ulla Idänpää-Heikkilä and Unto Häkkinen. Benchmarking the efficiency of hospital care. National Research and Development Centre for Welfare and Health. www.pcse.org/articles/index.asp?id=98.

England and Wales:
Public contributes to primary care decisions

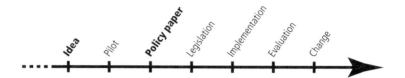

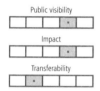

Public visibility

Impact

Transferability

Public opinion
tested with
questionnaires

Results derived
from questionnaire
responses

In January 2006, the British government issued a white paper with proposals for improving the integration of primary and secondary care. The aim of the document *Our Health, Our Care, Our Say* is the improvement of public access to primary care, because in the past health policies had concentrated more on secondary care.

In response to criticism from patients and primary caregivers, the government has developed a strategy to improve primary care and its integration with secondary care.

A feature of the new strategy has been public participation. More than 42,000 people, including members of specific groups such as patients and medical personnel, were asked about their needs in health care. In addition, a meeting was organized at which an invited audience of 1,000 could voice their interests and concerns. The analysis has identified three key criteria that people found most important for primary care: more control over their own care, increased support to maintain their own health, and quicker and easier access to higher-quality care that is more cost-effective.

On the basis of the results, the government announced that it would set up 125 readily accessible health centers and 50 community hospitals mainly for diagnostic activities. By mid-2006, people had been given more freedom in the choice of their general practitioner, and financial incentives were provided for GPs to offer more flexible surgery hours. In addition, responsibilities were reallocated between the NHS and the local authorities to improve cooperation; individual health check-ups with risk analysis were offered; more resources were made available for remote regions; individual care plans with fixed budgets were drawn up for the chronically ill; and a help hotline for medical personnel was set up.

By involving various interest groups, the government has largely No resistance ... avoided protests against the recommendations. But personnel working in secondary care did express concerns about the plans. Their concern is understandable, in view of a 5 percent shift of funds from secondary to primary care.

At the same time, experts are worried that NHS personnel are ... little enthusiasm showing signs of reform fatigue and as a result will show little enthusiasm for the proposals, despite the considerable increase in funding. A further problem is the tendency among participants to develop tunnel vision and, in association with this, the question of how primary carers and secondary carers can approach one another. Nevertheless, the shift toward stronger primary care is necessary to meet the population's future needs.

Sources and further reading:
Oliver, Adam. "Integrating community health and social care." *Health Policy Monitor*, April 2006. www.hpm.org/survey/uk/a7/3.

Department of Health. About Your health, your care, your say. www.dh.gov.uk/en/News/Yourhealthyourcareyoursay/DH_4136404.
Department of Health. Dozens of new doctors surgeries and health centres this year. http://www.dh.gov.uk/en/Publicationsandstatistics/Pressreleases/DH_4133098.
Department of Health. Our health, our care, our say. A new direction for community services. White Paper. London, 2006. www.dh.gov.uk/assetRoot/04/12/74/59/04127459.pdf.

Estonia: Family-doctor hotline 24/7

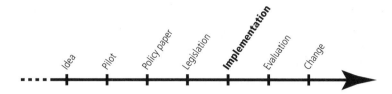

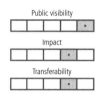

Public visibility

Impact

Transferability

1120: Direct help by phone

Improved access to primary care

Health insurance meets 80 percent of costs

Eighty-nine percent welcome hotline

Since August 2005, Estonian patients have had access round the clock to a central family doctor hotline. The objective of this project, initiated by the national health insurance fund, is to improve the availability of primary care. In the past there had been problems with securing access, particularly in remote regions and outside opening hours.

So far, about 9,000 callers a month have been making use of the hotline. When they dial 1120, they are directly connected with the medical staff on the helpline. In all, 10 general practitioners and 14 nurses are available in shifts, and they are able to deal with simple problems, arrange an appointment on the next day, call for an ambulance, or transfer the caller directly to an emergency section at a hospital. The call is free for the first five minutes as an incentive to use the hotline.

By introducing the hotline, the national health insurance is pursuing one of its strategic goals: to secure access to primary care by 2007 for the entire population and in particular for poorer people. With the 24-hour hotline, the social ministry and the health insurance service have ensured easy and rapid access to health care.

The preparations for the national hotline, which can also be contacted by Estonians in other countries, lasted three years. The winning bidder has received a contract to implement the hotline for the first three years, with the national health insurance fund meeting 80 percent of the costs.

In a survey conducted in 2003 by the national health insurance fund, 69 percent said they would welcome 24-hour access to a family doctor. 89 percent said that they would want to use a telephone service in an emergency. Surprisingly, some 20 percent of calls so far have come from Estonians living in neighboring Russia. In all, 95 percent of callers wanted to make an appointment with a general practitioner, whereas 5 percent wanted general information about health facilities.

The current service provider is also carrying out an evaluation of the actual use of the program and the satisfaction of patients and personnel. A cost-benefit analysis is also envisaged. Currently a telephone consultation costs 2.86 euros. The average cost of diagnostic treatment with a family doctor is about 6.39 euros. The system is not yet operating at full capacity, but if the number of calls increases in the coming year to the targeted 25,000, then the cost per call will be reduced.

More callers increases the benefit

The project is supported by representatives of all interest groups. Emergency services hope that the telephone hotline will reduce their own workload, and general practitioners, who at first feared dwindling numbers of patients, have now realized that the hotline is transferring patients to them. More advertising for the hotline is needed to increase the numbers of calls. The national health insurance system is considering advertising through family doctors, because they have direct contact with the potential callers.

Outcome depends on users

Sources and further reading:
Koppel, Agris, Sirje Vaask and Ain Aaviksoo. "Family Doctor Hotline." *Health Policy Monitor.* April 2006. www.hpm.org/survey/ee/a7/2.

Estonian Health Insurance Fund. Annual Report 2004. www.haigekassa.ee/files/eng_ehif_annual/aruanne_EN.pdf.
Ministry of Social Affairs. Strateegilised eesmärgid. www.sm.ee/est/pages/goproweb0057 [in Estonian].

Israel: Information brochure on long-term care insurance comes with the newspaper

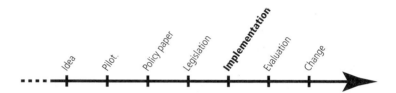

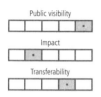

Public visibility

Impact

Transferability

Improved position when negotiating with insurers

Useful tips and ...

... simple explanations

With the goal of helping the population make the right choices when choosing an insurance policy for long-term care, in November 2005 the Israeli Ministry of Finance and the government's insurance comptroller published a brochure for the public on insurance for long-term care that was intended to be easy to understand. They hoped to strengthen the negotiating position of the population toward insurers and to draw attention to the possible disadvantages of certain forms of insurance.

Many people had not really been aware of their rights with regard to insurance for long-term care. When talking with insurance companies, potential clients had a difficult position because of the lack of transparency. The hope was that the information brochure would change things. In the opinion of the finance ministry and the auditing office, people with or without interest in insurance for long-term care ought to be able to talk with the insurance companies at eye level and then make a rational decision when concluding a contract.

The brochure also explains the three general options for insurance for long-term care: private insurance, collective insurance and insurance via the sickness fund. The most advantageous form of insurance varies with the situation of each individual. Because of the complicated regulation, people in the past often chose the simplest, but not necessarily the best, path.

The brochure was developed by ESHEL ("Association for Planning and Development for Services for the Elderly in Israel"), the Myers-JDC-Brookdale Institute and the finance ministry with the aim of reaching all parts of the population, which is why the three cooperation partners chose clear and simple language. The brochure presents the arguments in favor of taking out such insurance coverage, gives explanations about long-term care, tells of the public services provided for long-term care, and explains the concepts contained in an insurance policy and items that should be clarified before signing an insurance contract.

The brochure was included as a supplement in the most widely distributed weekend newspaper in Israel, and almost every household had a copy delivered to their home. The brochure has been published in all the common languages so that the entire population can receive the information.

In addition to the information campaign, the ministry and the insurance comptroller office hope to gain an improved public image. The project has received the backing of patients' organizations, which are hoping that there will be further targeted public campaigns in the future. But the insurance companies are hoping that the brochure will not have too much effect. They are worried about losses in market share and increased numbers of claims from existing policy holders as they become better informed about their entitlements.

In all, the action can be regarded as a success in view of the rapid and comprehensive distribution achieved.

Multilingual brochure for the entire population

Image boost for ministry and auditing office

Sources and further reading:
Gross, Revital, and Shuli Brammli-Greenberg. "Disseminating information on LTC insurance." *Health Policy Monitor*, April 2006. www.hpm.org/survey/is/a7/4.

National Insurance Institute. Long Term Care. www.btl.gov.il/English/btl_indx.asp?name=newbenefits/longterm.htm.

Austria: Law to protect the will of the individual

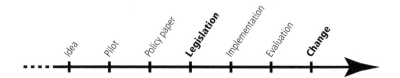

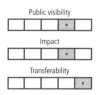

Public visibility

Impact

Transferability

Patients and doctors better protected

Four conditions determine validity

Debate since the 1990s

Since March 2006, Austrians have had the opportunity to draw up "patient dispositions" (living wills) on a legally binding basis. The disposition is intended to apply in situations in which the individual is no longer able to give informed consent. In such circumstances, doctors are not allowed to give the patient any treatment expressly forbidden in the living will. This typically includes measures such as dialysis, mechanical ventilation and artificial feeding.

The declared wishes of patients will now be respected in a situation in which they are unable to make decisions, particularly where modern life-extending techniques would lengthen suffering. Doctors will also benefit from legal security if they refrain from certain treatments for a patient in accordance with a living will.

Four conditions determine the validity of a living will. First, each treatment that is not to be carried out must be specified in the living will. Second, in order to ensure that the implications are understood, the patient must first consult a doctor, who must explain to the individual the nature of the medical treatment and the consequences of refusing it. The doctor must confirm with name, address and signature that the testator was of sound mind during the discussion. The living will only becomes binding in a third step, when it is certified by a judge, public notary, or a representative of a patients' association. It must be made clear that the living will can be revoked at any time. The fourth condition is that the living will must not be more than five years old.

Since the early 1990s, there has been an ongoing debate about the topic of patients' dispositions. The background to the discussions was the legal regulation of medically supervised suicides of severely ill people in the Netherlands and Switzerland.

After a parliamentary survey in 2001 under the title "Solidarity with the Dying," the health committee called for proposals for practical solutions regarding patients' dispositions. Between 2002 and

2003, a group of experts drew up guidelines aimed at providing patients and caregivers with greater security in the event of incapacity and death. In 2004, a draft was examined by the high court. As a result of this review, some alterations were necessary. The law was implemented in March 2006.

The fees for a patient's disposition currently amount to about 300 euros. So far there are no plans to use public funds to support socially disadvantaged people with the payment.

Disposition comes at a price

Another point is that there is no national register where living wills can be deposited. This means that doctors find it difficult to determine whether such a disposition exists, particularly if a patient has no relatives.

No central register

The opposition Social Democrats were the only party to vote against the bill, because they felt that there had not been enough political debate about the sensitive topic. They also asserted that the expense of the approach raises barriers. This point was also raised by experts' groups and various charitable organizations. The Red Cross and Caritas, for example, criticized the costs and the lack of a central register. But in general the two groups approve of the law.

Social Democrats vote against bill

Overall, experts expect positive effects from the increasing autonomy of the individual and an improved legal position for doctors. According to a survey, many respondents want to make use of the opportunity to draw up a living will. The costs (at least at their current level) do not seem to have any influence on the interest. But it remains to be seen how many people make use of their new right.

Positive effects expected

Sources and further reading:
Hofmarcher, Maria M., and Gerald Röhrling. "Living Will Law." *Health Policy Monitor,* April 2006. www.hpm.org/ survey/at/a7/2.

Gmeiner, Robert and Christian Kopetzki. Österreich auf dem Weg zu einem Patientenverfügungs-Gesetz? *Zeitschrift für Biopolitik,* (4) 2 2005. 67–75 [available only in German].

Health and aging

In the coming decades, there will be a growing demand in the OECD countries for financially viable, high-quality long-term care (see *Health Policy Developments*, issue 2, "Health and aging"). The reasons for this are increasing life expectancy and dwindling birth rates. The World Health Organization (WHO) estimates that from 1970 to 2025 the number of people over 60 years old worldwide will have more than doubled to 1.2 billion (WHO 2002). At the same time, the proportion of the "old old" is growing even more rapidly. Whereas in 1980 in OECD countries 36.1 million people (out of a total of 966.6 million) were between 65 and 69 years old, the number is predicted to rise by 2025 to 77.4 million (of 1.33 billion). Among persons older than 85, the rise is even greater: from 7.1 million in 1980 to a predicted 69.5 million in 2025 (OECD 2007).

These developments present a number of challenges for long-term care policies. The coordination of various health and social services is one of the key tasks. Interface problems in the coordination of services for acute needs, rehabilitation, and health care (see report on the Netherlands on page 132 and on Singapore on page 135) can lead not only to unsatisfactory results for the patients but also to an inefficient deployment of resources within the healthcare and long-term care systems (OECD 2005: 3).

The further development of care to a coordinated system is of crucial importance for patients who are cared for at home or in communal institutions. Measures that allow elderly people to stay at home as long as possible can be an essential contribution to improving the situation for many older people in need of care (OECD 2005) (see report on New Zealand on page 137).

Keeping the elderly at home

Promoting an
active way of life
to preserve health
The concept of active aging was established by the WHO in the second half of the 1990s. It refers to supporting self-responsibility, the creation of an age-appropriate environment and the encouragement of solidarity between generations. The promotion of active aging makes sense from the perspective both of health policy and of economics, because the costs for care are reduced when people stay healthier longer (WHO 2005).

The ability to live an active life in old age depends on various factors. First, it is linked to the skills, capabilities and interests of the person; second, it depends on his material and social security and his spatial, social and infrastructural setting; and third, it reflects attitudes in society about the elderly (WHO 2005: 10).

The isolation of old people and their frequent lack of motivation to take up new activities make it necessary to take new initiatives to activate them. The usual approach is to create various opportunities for leisure and health-promotion activities for the elderly (WHO 2005) (see report on Israel on page 141).

For people who are cared for at home, several OECD countries have developed a portfolio of cash-benefit programs over the past 10 years, so that those needing care and their families can make a choice about care that meets their particular needs. These programs take various forms: (1) care budgets for the engagement of home care personnel by the "consumer" (i.e., the person needing care); (2) payments to the person needing care, who can then choose how to spend the money; and (3) direct payments to private caregivers in the form of an income subsidy (OECD 2005).

With personal budgets and self-determined engagement of home care personnel, many (but not all) older people are in a position to hire a personal helper, who may also be a relative. The income supports paid to private caring personnel serve a dual purpose: They increase flexibility and they mobilize (or at least maintain) a larger pool of caregivers. The result is that elderly people are able to remain in their own surroundings longer. At the same time, the need for expensive institutional care is reduced.

Germany, Japan, Luxembourg and Austria are among the countries that have decided to introduce new, more or less comprehensive insurance for long-term care. With the exception of Austria, these are social insurance programs based on the model for healthcare funding in these countries—those who are insured

130

have an entitlement to care when in need. The first country to introduce such a system was the Netherlands, back in 1968. This system was recently reformed twice, first in 2003 when the benefit categories were redefined, and again in 2006 when responsibilities between health insurers and local authorities were redefined (see page 132). Some countries (e.g., in Scandinavia) have tax-funded services; others, to keep costs down, have retained programs that provide support only for the needy (e.g., Australia and the United Kingdom).

Sources and further reading:
OECD. Long-term care for older people. Paris: OECD Publishing, 2005.
OECD. Society at a Glance. OECD. Social Indicators 2006 Edition. Paris: OECD Publishing, 2007.
United Nations Population Division, DESA. World Population Prospects. The 2006 Revision. www.un.org/esa/population/publications/wpp2006/wpp2006_ageing.pdf.
World Health Organization. Active Ageing. A Policy Framework. Geneva, 2002. www.euro.who.int/document/hea/eactagepolframe.pdf.
World Helath Organization. Gesundes Altern. Aufsuchende Aktivierung älterer Menschen. Kopenhagen 2005. www.euro.who.int/document/hea/gesundes_altern_g.pdf.

The Netherlands: Decentralization of responsibility for health-related social benefits

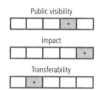

Public visibility

Impact

Transferability

The Law for Social Support (Wet maatschappelijke ondersteuning, or WMO) came into force in 2006. It transfers responsibility for certain health-related social services, including family support (home care such as housework, basic health support, hygiene) from the first pillar of the Dutch health insurance system for "exceptional medical expenses" (Algemene Wet Bijzondere Ziektekosten, or AWBZ) to the local authorities. This reflects the judgment that local authorities are better placed than health insurers to organize family support and integrated nursing care for ill and weak elderly people.

Supporting informal help …

With the WMO, policymakers are pursuing several health-related and municipal goals. One goal is to make users of health-related social services more independent from public care. If possible, health-related social services should be organized at the private level, for example in the form of informal help. Patients are entitled to state-organized social support only when no other opportunities are available.

… and integration of social care

A second goal is the integration of social care in other public services such as neighborhood help and Meals on Wheels. In the opinion of the government, local authorities are more competent than health insurers to offer an integrated package of social support services. Opponents are worried that WMO has been introduced as a vehicle for further cuts in health-related social services. However, this is expressively denied by the government.

WMO supports independent lifestyles

The WMO offers a new institutional framework for decentralizing the provision of health-related social services. Local authorities are regarded in the Netherlands as the institutions best suited to provide an integrated range of social services in home surroundings for people needing help and nursing care so that they can live independently for as long as possible.

132

The WMO should be seen in the context of the health insurance reform of 2006 and the fundamental political discussion about the future of the AWBZ insurance. Before the WMO, health-related social services fell under the AWBZ. The AWBZ was originally intended to cover unusually high medical costs, mainly for long-term care. However, since the introduction of the law in 1968, more and more services that had little or nothing to do with long-term care or exceptional medical expenditure were added to the AWBZ benefit basket.

AWBZ vs. WMO: Separation of nursing care and social services

The WMO not only creates an institutional framework for integrated care at the level of the local authorities but is also a political instrument to remove from the AWBZ benefit basket all those services that do not conform to the goal of insurance for long-term care for the entire population (see issue 4, "Organizational reform").

Institutional conditions and rearrangement of the benefits catalog

The Balkenende government has initiated the WMO with the support of the health ministry. The hope is that the law will contribute to solving the funding problems of the AWBZ and make it possible to achieve a better level of integrated care at the community level. But local authorities are ambivalent about the new law. On the one hand, they support the WMO, because it increases their scope for action. On the other hand, they are worried that the national government will misuse the WMO to cut expenditures for social services.

Local authorities worried about cuts in social services

Health insurers have adopted a neutral stance. Their primary concern is the smooth organizational transfer of responsibilities. Providers of social services have not really come out in support of the law. It is in their interest to have stable, long-term relationships with the health insurers. Local authorities are a volatile element for them, because as a result of EU legislation they will have to put social services out for tender. The providers are worried that competition from other EU member states could lead to massive losses in revenues, or in the worst case even to the bankruptcy of the Dutch service providers.

Dutch providers worried by the EU single market

Patient organizations have also not approved of the law. They worry about cuts in expenditures. They see the risk that shifting responsibility for social services from the health insurers to the local authorities will mean that clients will lose their entitlement of social assistance.

Social services: legal entitlement or commodity? A very important concern in the legislature's debate was how to secure legal entitlement to social services under the new regulations. Whereas the AWBZ provided a legal right to social support if the client met specific criteria, the WMO does not include this right. Various political parties have already announced that this right to social services would be reintroduced under a new government, but it remains to be seen whether this would actually be put into practice.

Sources and further reading:
Maarse, Hans. "Law on Social Support." *Health Policy Monitor,* October 2006. www.hpm.org/survey/nl/a8/1.

Busse, Reinhard, Ewout van Ginneken, Jonas Schreyögg and Wendy Wisbaum. The health care system and reform in the Netherlands. *Euro Observer. Newsletter of the European Observatory on Health Systems and Policies* (7) 1: 6-8, 2005. www.euro.who.int/document/obs/euro observer7_1.pdf.

College voor Zorgverzekeringen (Health Care Insurance Board of the Netherlands). www.cvz.nl.

van Ginneken, Ewout. "Health Insurance Reform in the Netherlands." *Health Policy Monitor,* March 2006. http://www.hpm.org/survey/de/a6/1.

Ministry of Health, Welfare and Sport. www.minvws.nl/en

Zogverzezekaars Nederland (sector organization representing the providers of care insurance in the Netherlands). www.zn.nl.

Singapore: Integration of acute medical care, inpatient recovery and rehabilitation care

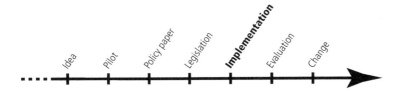

St. Andrew's Community Hospital (SACH) was opened in April 2005. It was the first community hospital in the direct vicinity of a general acute hospital, the Changi General Hospital. The proximity of the acute hospital and a hospital with inpatient recovery and rehabilitation care makes it easier to coordinate and integrate care of patients. Among other things, it also allows the two institutions to share services and medical equipment such as cardiology, laboratories, nutritional advice and medical care.

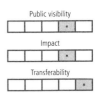

Older patients in particular are often healthy enough to be released from an acute hospital but too ill to care for themselves alone at home. They need more care and treatment in institutions that offer post-acute or step-down care in order to make it easier for them to reintegrate themselves into their home. In Singapore, community hospitals are step-down institutions offering inpatient recovery and rehabilitation care. An example is the SACH which belongs to the St. Andrew's Mission Hospital, a welfare organization founded in 1913. SACH has provided affordable sub-acute and step-down nursing care since 1992.

In view of the growing need for nursing care for the elderly in the coming decades, the health ministry is trying to establish the right organizational and financial structures. The opening of the new facilities of the 200-bed SACH in October 2006 shows a new development: a community hospital offering affordable, limited services and located close to an acute hospital.

Step-down care is often expensive for patients because it is extended over a relatively long period. Addressing this problem, the government supports needy elderly people, on the basis of an income examination, by a means trust that was introduced in 2000.

St. Andrew's Community Hospital (SACH)

Side by side: community and general hospitals

It is expected that patients will find it easier and less stressful to move from one institution to the other. In addition, less time is lost if patients and their relatives are uncertain about whether the patient should be moved to a community hospital. The St. Andrew's Community Hospital offers rehabilitative care for patients with an average age of 75 years. These inpatient services have the objective of improving the patients' condition so that they can return home.

The annual expenditure of the 14-year-old community hospital amounts to SGD 7 million (3.5 million euros), of which 45 percent is covered by state supplements and subsidies and 30 percent by the patients. With 80 to 85 patients, this means that an average of SGD 70 (35 euros) per day must be received per patient. Because of the growing demand, the hospital opened three additional wards in 2006. This increased the capacity by 90 beds, so that the annual expenditure will probably increase to SGD 13.5 million (6.75 million euros).

The health ministry is currently working on a financial plan that will allow patients needing inpatient rehabilitation services to receive more subsidies in the future. Alterations seem necessary in particular because of two inappropriate incentives in the current funding system. At the moment, patients stay longer in the (acute-care) hospitals than necessary because it is less expensive than moving to a step-down institution. A second aspect is the financial imbalance between care in care homes and in the reorganized community hospitals. Currently, 80 percent of patients in care homes receive some form of state support, compared to only 50 percent of those in community hospitals.

Sources and further reading:
Lim, Meng Kin. "Integrating acute and step-down elderly care". *Health Policy Monitor*, October 2006. www.hpm. org/survey/sg/a8/2.

Ministry of Health Singapore: www.moh.gov.sg/corp/ elderlycare/subsidies/intro.do.

New Zealand: Aging in place—projects and evaluation

In New Zealand elderly people are being encouraged to remain in their trusted surroundings and neighborhood by means of two state programs, the Health of Older People Strategy (2002) and the New Zealand Positive Ageing Strategy (2001). Here we look at the first of these strategies, which is to be implemented by the District Health Boards (DHBs) until 2010. In 2006, three pilot programs supporting aging in place were evaluated in a project called ASPIRE (Assessment of Services Promoting Independence and Recovery in Elders).

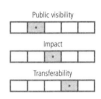

The Health of Older People Strategy aims to enable the elderly to make independent decisions regarding their health and well-being in their familiar social environment for as long as possible. They will receive support from coordinated health and disability programs. A core goal of the strategy is to provide older people with timely access to primary health services, thereby making it possible for the elderly to proactively preserve and improve their health and mobility. This strategy allows them to stay in their home surroundings for as long as possible.

Goal of promoting the independence of elderly people

The strategy originated in cooperation between the Ministry of Health and an advisory group of experts, older people and local authorities throughout New Zealand. Three pilot programs were developed regionally in a joint process with all relevant stakeholders. Some features of the programs are derived from similar initiatives in other countries. The implementation of the strategy is the responsibility of the health ministry and the DHBs.

Joint development of programs

After the publication of the draft strategy in 2001, the public had two months (until September 2001) to inform themselves about the draft and comment on it. In view of the considerable interest, the deadline was extended to January 2002. The reactions—many of which related to the implementation and details of the objectives—were very positive. However, worries were ex-

Integration of stakeholders in strategy development

pressed that older people were not sufficiently integrated into the advisory experts' group. Some institutional providers of long-term care were also against the idea of encouraging people to stay in their own homes, because in many regions home nursing care services were not very well developed and these people could not be provided with adequate support.

Evaluation results form the basis for more programs
ASPIRE is part of the "Health of Older People Information Plan: Directions to 2010 and Beyond" (2006). The results of the ASPIRE evaluation underpin the development of performance indicators for authority programs at the community level. The health ministry will observe the implementation of the strategy by the DHBs in accordance with its annual plans and carry out examinations in a three-year rhythm.

Evaluation of three projects
The Ministry of Health commissioned the University of Auckland with the evaluation of the three pilot programs. In the first part of the evaluation (Parsons et al. 2006), the clinical effectiveness of the projects investigated. The second part covers the costs of the measures.

The three projects evaluated—COSE, PIP and Community FIRST—are concerned with structural aspects, specifically avoiding an oversupply of care, and also the specificity of the measures, that is, the provision of care for older people appropriate to their needs.

1. The COSE (Coordination of Services for Elderly) initiative identifies care needs for elderly people and coordinates services to avoid duplication. A care coordinator works with the general practitioner to identify a person's nursing-care needs, then looks for main and voluntary offers for nursing care and home services in the locality and coordinates the individual care packets.

2. PIP (Promoting Independence Programme) organizes the older person's path through the rehabilitation process as individual case management. Elderly patients are provided with particularly intensive care after a stay in hospital: up to 12 months in a rehabilitation clinic and then up to 12 months at home. The goal of this program is the complete recovery of the elderly patients, so that they will be able to live in their home again as independently as possible. The program was developed by a long-term care service in cooperation with a District Health Board.

138

3. Community FIRST (Flexible Integrated Restorative Teams) has as its goal the specific support of older people with a need for high levels of complex care in their home. The program covers individual care management, a flexible care structure and flat-rate funding. Care can be adapted to meet the patient's daily needs. A patient whose state of health worsens can temporarily be moved to a nursing home. When the situation improves, the patient can return home and will receive support for social reintegration. FIRST is a cooperation project between a provider of home nursing care, a District Health Board and the Ministry of Health.

ASPIRE is a meta-analysis of three random samples of the Ageing in Place initiatives. In each sample, patients were allocated randomly to the group receiving conventional care and the Ageing in Place group. Five hundred and sixty-nine participants were included in the three groups. *Randomized evaluation studies*

The conclusion from the evaluation is that elderly people needing high levels of complex care, who otherwise would be admitted to a nursing home, can safely remain in their home if appropriate nursing care is provided. Among other things, the ASPIRE analyses have shown that the Ageing in Place pilot projects are effective. The people receiving care were admitted to the hospital less frequently and the mortality rate was lower than with conventional nursing care provisions. At the same time, the burden on caregivers is not greater than it is with conventional services. *Positive results of the evaluation*

Whether the projects will be extended to cover all New Zealand depends on several factors. If the need for support is not equally large in all District Health Boards, there is a risk of regionally unequal access to home care. In addition, there is a risk that elderly patients will be refused access to nursing homes and hospitals even though they need to be admitted. Hasty and uncontrolled introduction of the homecare program could also lead to unrecognized stress on members of the caring family, who may face excessive demands. In addition to nursing care, there are many other factors influencing independence in old age: inner attitudes, family, home environment, transportation possibilities, and access to public institutions. If these aspects are not consid- *Possible constraints* ered part of a coordinated and integrated package, it is unlikely that the introduction or extension of the Ageing in Place strategies will meet the needs of older people and their families.

Positive conclusions
The successful implementation of the Ageing in Place programs at the national level will require a national focus, suitable funding, and well-established cooperation among the sectors. The policy is pointing in the right direction, but it seems very ambitious in view of the current scope and quality of homecare services.

Domestic nursing care services are still not yet very widespread in New Zealand. And those that are available are frequently of rather poor quality, with a poorly paid, undertrained workforce. Considerable investments would be needed to develop the sector to the point that a substantially larger number of older people could remain in their home and receive care there.

Sources and further reading:
Ramage, Carol. "Evaluation of strategies for 'Ageing in Place.'" *Health Policy Monitor,* October 2006. www.hpm. org/survey/nz/a8/5.

Parsons, Matthews, et al. An Economic Evaluation of the Assessment of Services Promoting Independence and Recovery in Elders (ASPIRE). Auckland: UniServices Limited, 2006.
Ministry of Health. Key findings of research trial to improve outcomes for older people released. Media Release, September 26, 2006. www.moh.govt.nz/moh.nsf/by+ unid/672F0E6427851E4DCC2571F5000F8ECE?Open.
Dalziel, Lianne. The New Zealand Positive Ageing Strategy. Wellington: Ministry of Social Policy, 2001. www. osc.govt.nz.
Dwyer, Maire, Alison Gray and Margery Renwick. Factors affecting the ability of older people to live independently. A report for the International Year of Older Persons 1999. Wellington: Ministry Of Social Policy, 2000. www.osc.govt.nz.

Dyson, Ruth. Health of Older People Strategy: Health Sector Action to 2010 to Support Positive Ageing. Wellington: Ministry of Health, 2002. www.moh.govt.nz/publi cations/hops.

Ministry of Health. Health of Older People information Strategic Plan. Directions to 2010 and beyond. Wellington, 2006. www.moh.govt.nz/moh.nsf/238fd5fb4fd0518 44c256669006aed57/6bc2def365392e0ecc257145007e7 ecd?OpenDocument.

The New Zealand Institute of Economic Research (NZIER). Ageing New Zealand Health and Disability Services: Demand Projections and Workforce Implications 2001– 2021. A discussion document. Wellington: Ministry of Health, 2004. www.moh.govt.nz/moh.nsf/0/E6EE108 D0901CAD8CC256F73000F1F9A/$File/nzierreportage ingnzandhealthanddisabilityservices.pdf.

Israel: Keeping the elderly fit and healthy

To support elderly people, a pilot project was carried out with the goals of mobilizing the physical and mental health of elderly people and also sensitizing physicians to the special health needs and health risks faced by elderly people. The regional pilot trials were carried out in the central district of the Maccabi health service. Maccabi is the second-largest of the four Israeli health insurers, providing health services through a network of 3,500 physicians in over 150 branches and clinics.

The program consists of six measures. Three are directed at medical interventions and prevention measures, or both. Three are directed at physical fitness. The measures are vaccinations against

Prevention
targeted at the
needs of elderly
people

flu and pneumonia, hearing and sight screening tests (with treatment if necessary), observation of eating behavior (with adjustments if necessary), introduction to and advice about physical activity, care after falls, and advice about the avoidance of falls.

The program begins with a meeting between a doctor and the elderly patient to register the patient's health status and develop an appropriate care plan. The elderly patients and their general practitioners also receive separate oral introductions to prevention and health promotion as well as documentation on this topic. Moreover, the elderly people take part in sports groups paid for by the health insurer.

The program was initiated by the Association for Planning and Development for Services for the Elderly in Israel (*ESHEL*) and the Maccabi Health Services health insurance fund, which covers about 24 percent of the population. ESHEL is an association that is particularly active on behalf of the elderly.

The objective of ESHEL is to set up a countrywide program for health promotion for elderly people. It cooperates with all those partners who have the same interests and are willing to cooperate. Health insurance funds are the preferred partner for ESHEL because they have not only the same goals but also the infrastructure necessary to implement this program. They also can contact the target groups.

Before the development of the program, discussions had taken place for two years between Maccabi and ESHEL. Representatives of the geriatric section of the health ministry also took part. They were mainly interested in the development of prevention and health promotion programs for elderly people. The topics of these discussions were the feasibility of possible programs as well as the selection of the most relevant health indicators for older people, on which the program should concentrate. This discussion was based on American and Canadian reports from working groups on prevention.

ESHEL and the geriatric section of the health ministry have the common goal of extending health promotion for elderly people. They can implement this goal to some extent with the pilot project. Both have participated actively in planning and implementing the program and securing funding. For Maccabi, the program offers an opportunity to promote health maintenance for the elderly while controlling costs and enhancing the satisfaction of the participants.

The program was evaluated by the Myers-JDC-Brookdale Institute. Designed as a case-control study, the evaluation took into account both process factors and outcome parameters. There were two control groups: elderly people who did not take part in the program themselves but whose doctors did, and elderly people treated by doctors in the same district not directly involved in the program. The doctors were questioned in focus groups; the patients were interviewed by telephone. Additional data was obtained from administrative records, for example of flu infections and hospital admissions.

Evaluation in the form of scientific monitoring

The reputation of the health insurance fund has been enhanced. It is also expected that the preventive measures and the early recognition of risks and diseases will reduce the subsequent use of medical services such as hospital stays. The district directors saw the inclusion of their districts in the pilot program as proof of their willingness to embrace innovation and an opportunity to demonstrate their willingness to improve. The head of the geriatric section of the health ministry saw an opportunity to demonstrate a willingness to act.

Program benefits all stakeholders

The Maccabi general practitioners were on the whole not opposed to the program, because during the pilot phase participation in the program was offered to qualified doctors who were willing to cooperate with the district management of the health insurer. The elderly people, finally, were much more intensively cared for and felt much better treated by their doctors and the health insurance than before the project.

The Maccabi community nurses were dissatisfied because they had not been involved in the program. In their view, they are the ones who have the most to do with caring for the elderly and who also play a key role in health promotion. Therefore the community nurses demand that in the future they be integrated more deeply into the program.

Nurses demand increased involvement

The patient interviews reveal an increase in the number of prevention and health promotion programs in the six areas selected for the pilot program. The management of the health insurer had expected to observe more outcome results such as a decline in the numbers of hospital admissions and flu infections.

Results of patient interviews: too soon to tell

It was not possible to demonstrate this because the effect of the program could not be isolated.

The results show that for the elderly people in the experimental group and the first control group (patients do not take part in the pilot project, but their doctor does), sight and hearing tests were carried out more frequently, as were vaccinations against pneumonia. The results of the second control group (neither patient nor doctor participate in the pilot project) showed no changes.

Elderly people in the experimental and first control groups also reported more frequently that the doctor asked them whether they had had a hearing or sight test, and also whether they had fallen recently. The number of elderly people who reported that the doctor had asked them about weight changes and spoken with them about the importance of physical fitness only showed an increase in the experimental group.

Benefits also for elderly people who do not take part

The results show that the doctors make use of what they have learned in the pilot program for all patients, not just those enrolled in the pilot program. These results correspond with the assessments of the doctors as expressed in the focus group discussions, in which they confirmed that the pilot program had raised their general level of awareness about the needs of elderly people. They reported that they paid more attention to developments and events such as weight loss and falls in elderly people than before the pilot project.

No long-term effects for doctors and patients

Soon after the pilot program was completed, doctors reported that their enthusiasm had declined. This indicates that the program cannot be implemented in its present form without some alterations. The evaluation showed that if the doctors are to pay special attention to older patients, they need more time for each patient than was provided for in the program. Patients also reported that their enthusiasm, for example to take part in sports courses, declined considerably after the end of the program.

Positive results expected for countrywide implementation

Overall, the evaluation showed that the program had considerable potential to improve the quality of care and the health of elderly people, as well as their satisfaction and their participation. It is expected that countrywide introduction of the program would lead to an improvement in the health of elderly people. The program is particularly promising when it comes to mobilizing older

144

people with lower levels of education and less knowledge about healthful living. Regarding the medical parameters, it is expected that countrywide introduction, with vaccinations and counseling, would lead to a decline in hospital admissions due to pneumonia and hip fractures.

Sources and further reading:
Bentur, Netta. "Health Promotion Project for the Elderly." *Health Policy Monitor,* October 2006. www.hpm.org/survey/is/a8/2.

Bentur, Netta, Diane Citron and Svetlana Chekkemir. Prevention and health promotion among the elderly in the community. An evaluation study. Myers-JDC-Brookdale research report (forthcoming, in Hebrew with English abstract).

Coping with future shortages of health professionals

The current discussion about health professionals in industrialized countries is concentrated mainly on three topics: quality and interfaces, numbers in relation to requirements, and further qualification. The lack of well-organized interfaces between the various sectors, and in particular between doctors and nursing staff, leads to inefficiencies that need to be minimized. Another factor is the number of nursing staff in relation to the numbers of people needing care.

The number of general practitioners relative to the size of the population has risen slowly but steadily in most OECD countries in recent decades. Currently, there are on average 3.2 doctors per 1,000 inhabitants. Nevertheless, in many OECD countries concerns are growing about undersupply, especially of general practitioners in rural areas. For example, in the United States, Great Britain, New Zealand and Australia, attempts are being made to solve the problem by extending the responsibilities of nursing staff with the introduction of nurse practitioners. **Numbers of doctors increasing, distribution uneven**

Nurse practitioners are registered nurses who have completed an additional training course. In addition, they have had special training about frequent complaints and chronic conditions. They ease the workload of doctors by carrying out certain tasks such as prescribing some pharmaceutical products and less expensive treatments. Nurse practitioners concentrate on how patients feel and how an illness is affecting their lives and the lives of their dependents (see reports on Germany on page 151 and on New Zealand on page 154 as well as report from the Netherlands in *Health Policy Developments,* issue 2). **Interface between doctor and nurse: nurse practitioners**

The second approach to resolving the disparity between growing numbers of patients needing health care and trained care personnel is to recruit staff from other countries. Statistics available about the migration of personnel are most likely incomplete, but an idea of migration within the European Union is given in table 2.

Table 2: Migration of nurses within the EU in 2000

Country	Number of nurses who have received a work permit in another EU country
Portugal	1,611
Ireland	1,097
Sweden	231
Italy	138
Spain	128–133
The Netherlands	126
Austria	99
Germany	88
Denmark	17
Finland	4

Source: Buchan 2006

However, migration within the European Union accounts only for a small part of the migration movements in most member states, which have tended to recruit personnel from countries outside the European Union.

Healthcare personnel have different reasons for migrating. Those who emigrate permanently cite reasons such as the wish to improve their living standard, the better career possibilities offered, and the emigration of their partners. Personnel who leave their native country for a limited period may be making use of the opportunity to obtain further qualifications. They also may have only been offered a limited contract in the host country and hope the experience will improve their job prospects when they return home. Others are making use of their qualifications as a way of financing a stay abroad (Buchan 2006).

According to figures from the World Health Organization (WHO), the majority of nursing staff working outside their own country come from the Philippines. Officially there are assumed to be some 250,000 nurses from this country working abroad.

They travel to Europe, Africa and South and North America, and since September 2006 also to Japan (see page 159). Philippine nurses have a very good reputation because of their social skills and ability to speak English. The incentive for them to leave their native country is primarily the much higher wages abroad. Nurses in the Philippines earn about US $200 a month. Nursing staff in Great Britain, for example, can earn about $1,800 a month (Sison 2002).

A different approach to internationalization has been adopted in Singapore (see page 171). To save personnel, x-ray images are now no longer analyzed in Singapore, but in India. Within a few seconds of being taken in Singapore, the x-ray images are sent to India with the assistance of modern information technology and analyzed by an expert there; the findings are then sent back to Singapore. This has made it possible to reduce the time between the x-ray being taken and the results becoming available from two weeks to a few hours. The model for Singapore in this case was the United States, where teleradiology is used to obtain analyses from India for night-time emergency cases. **International outsourcing**

Attempts were originally also made in Canada to make up for the shortage of doctors by encouraging foreign physicians to come to work in the country. Because this strategy gave rise to massive protests, efforts are now concentrated on national strategies. For example, Canada has set up a 10-year plan for a complete restructuring of medical training, coupled with an increase in the numbers of students. In addition, new cross-sectoral professional groups will be created so that personnel can be employed more flexibly (see page 161). The Australian government has also developed a 10-year plan to systematically tackle the shortages of personnel. In addition to increasing the numbers of students, other medical personnel will take over duties from doctors by allowing them access to public finances through Medicare (see page 166). Slovenia is also attempting to counter a foreseeable shortage of medical personnel—of nurses in the case of Slovenia—through long-term planning (see page 168). **Medical training**

France has put together a package of measures at various levels to counteract the marked differences in health care between rural and urban areas and to ensure a high quality of care. The government has organized a system made up of financial, legal **France puts package of measures together**

149

and training measures (see page 163). England and Wales have also chosen financial incentives. Because of the low salary potential for dentists in England and Wales, the NHS has encountered recruiting problems. Income was very unpredictable because of high co-payments for patients; the costs of dental surgeries could hardly be covered, and as a result dentists were no longer keen to work within the NHS. Now fundamental reforms have been introduced to improve working conditions and make it easier for patients to access services by lowering co-payments. Dentists are no longer paid for individual services but receive one of three flat-rated fees for each treatment (see page 169).

Sources and further reading:
Buchan, James. Migration of health workers in Europe. Policy problem or policy solution? In *Human resources for health in Europe,* edited by Carl-Ardy Dubois, Martin McKee and Ellen Nolte. European Observatory on Health Systems and Policies. Maidenhead: Open University Press, 2006: 41–62. www.euro.who.int/document/e879 23_4.pdf.

European Commission, Working Party Health Systems. European mobility of medical and nursing workforce. Presentation, DG Sanco C–2. March 25, 2004. http:// ec.europa.eu/health/ph_information/implement/wp/ systems/docs/ev_20040325_co01_en.pdf.

Advisory Council for the Concerted Action in Health Care. *Report 2000/2001. Appropriateness and Efficiency. Vol. III: Overuse, Underuse and Misuse. III. 3. Need, Appropriate Care, Overuse, Underuse and Misuse.* www.svr-gesundheit. de/Gutachten/Gutacht01/Kurzf-engl01.pdf.

Sison, Marites. Philippinische Krankenpfleger suchen ihr Glück im Ausland. *Ärzte Zeitung. 30.8.2002.* www.aerzte zeitung.de/docs/2002/08/30/154a1101.asp [available only in German].

Germany: Improving healthcare structures with nurse practitioners

Under the name AGnES, the Institute for Community Medicine of the University of Greifswald is currently carrying out several pilot projects in various parts of eastern Germany. The acronym AGnES is also an intentional reference to the first name of a well-known nurse in an East German television series (Korzilius and Rabbata 2006). In the model project in Mecklenburg-West Pomerania, so-called community nurses pay house visits and are responsible for basic primary care. The nursing personnel are supported by eHealth equipment. In rural regions with a relatively low density of general practitioners and long distances between patients, it is intended to ease the burden on family doctors and provide patients with improved access to (basic) medical care.

The profession of community nurse equals the nurse practitioner of other countries. It is an extension of the duties of a nurse to include tasks (such as taking blood samples and carrying out diagnostic tests) that are usually the responsibility of doctors or members of other professions. If the strategy is introduced on a broader scale, it will have a fundamental influence on the structures of the German health system.

Support for doctors and patients

For the qualification of community nurses, the University of Greifswald has developed a special training program. Hospital nurses will acquire necessary additional knowledge by observing the activities of general practitioners, in particular in the treatment of the chronically ill, and learn how to use the eHealth equipment.

In Brandenburg, the University of Greifswald is supporting the largest project of this type with 50,000 euros per year. The main portion of the funding is provided by the European Social Funds and the Brandenburg Ministry of Health, each with 300,000 euros per year. The two-year project began in July 2006. If it proves suc-

Funding and continuation

cessful, nurse practitioners will become established as an element of the health structures in Brandenburg. Because a smaller project in Mecklenburg-West Pomerania in 2005 led to positive results, the provincial government of this federal state is planning to introduce nurse practitioners throughout the state. Other federal states are considering whether to introduce similar projects.

Controversy about occupational status of nurse practitioners

The initiators of the pilot project envisage nurse practitioners being employees of a general practitioner. Such an arrangement will foster close links between doctor and nurse and ensure that there is a clear chain of responsibility. A second possibility is the nurse being employed by a social insurance body that can enter into contracts with general practitioners. Such an arrangement would be a fundamental transformation in financing structures, because care services are currently covered mainly by separate nursing care insurance and not by statutory health insurance. The final decision lies with the Federal Joint Committee (G-BA), which is made up of representatives of the health insurers, service providers and patient organizations. The committee defines the ambulatory service catalogue and its financing.

Financing of a nationwide introduction is unclear

The long-term financing of nurse practitioners as an element of the German health system is still a matter of debate. There are discussions about whether the main portion of the funding should be provided from health insurance payments to medical associations or come directly from the health insurances in addition to payments to the provider of services.

Social associations and long-term care facilities fear for jobs ...

There is strong opposition to the model of community nurses from social associations and institutions providing long-term care. They see community nurses as publicly subsidized competition to existing care facilities and fear the loss of jobs in this sector. In their eyes, the introduction of community nurses in the ambulatory care sector is inefficient and expensive. The initiators of the AGnES project argue that nurse practitioners will not replace social help institutions and long-term nursing care, but rather will be able to offer medical care as required.

... but approve of more rights and responsibilities for nurses

In principle, the social associations and institutions of long-term care favor allowing other professions in the health system to carry out activities previously the sole responsibility of doctors. But instead of introducing community nurses, they argue that doctors should be allowed to transfer basic medical services to

152

staff working for the social associations and long-term care facilities.

The responses of the doctors' associations have varied widely. Some representatives in eastern Germany support the project. They see the introduction of nurse practitioners as a way of easing the load on rural doctors. But they insist that the community nurses should be directly employed by the general practitioner and that they should act only on the instructions of the doctor responsible. Other representatives of doctors' associations emphasize that nurse practitioners cannot replace general practitioners and complain that the project is only obscuring the real problem of the dwindling numbers of doctors in rural areas. They fear a loss of quality of medical care and see a risk that patients will pay fewer visits to the doctor.

Opinions vary among doctors

The German government views the nurse practitioners positively and has emphasized its intention to continue cooperation and further integration of the various professions in the health system. They see an opportunity in this to strengthen integrated care and to lower costs, because calculations show that a nurse practitioner only generates one third of the costs of a general practitioner. The state governments and the University of Greifswald have drawn a positive conclusion from the AGnES projects.

Approval from national and state governments

Given the introduction of appropriate training for the nurse practitioners, the quality of health care would not decline. There is a positive effect on equality of access to health care, with potential improvements especially for old and ill patients in rural areas. Since it is much less expensive to employ a nurse practitioner than a general practitioner, the transfer of basic medical services to the community nurses is highly cost-effective.

Positive overall evaluation of the pilot projects

Therefore, government representatives support the inclusion of the nurse practitioner in the general health system. At the regional level, the doctors' organization, the social associations, and the long-term care institutions are planning a joint commission to resolve the dispute and to find a common standpoint, concerning, among other matters, financing and occupational status.

Sources and further reading:
Blum, Kerstin. "Nurse practitioners in eastern Germany." *Health Policy Monitor*, October 2006. www.hpm.org/survey/ger/a8/1.

Informationsdienst Wissenschaft. 1000. Hausbesuch für Gemeindeschwester AGnES. Pressemitteilung. Ernst-Moritz-Arndt-Universität Greifswald, 27.02.2007. http://idw-online.de/pages/de/news197798 [available only in German].
Korzilius, Heike, and Samir Rabbata. Gemeindeschwestern. Geheimwaffe gegen Überlastung und Unterversorgung. *Deutsches Ärzteblatt* (103) 44: A-2926, 03.11. 2006. www.aerzteblatt.de/v4/archiv/artikel.asp?id=53297 [available only in German].

New Zealand: Further development of nursing care

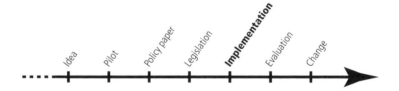

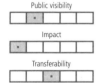

The reorganization of nursing care services in New Zealand began in 1998. Intermediate steps took the form of a New Zealand Primary Health Care Strategy in 2001, the formation of an Expert Advisory Group in 2003, the provision of funds for the development of innovative models of nursing care, and the extension of funds by the government to include study grants for the further training of qualified nursing personnel who are active in basic nursing care. In 2006, the reorganization of nursing care took a step forward. This reorientation is aimed at a broader focus of public health with the emphasis on prevention and health promotion. The second part is to offer a broader spectrum of nursing care services.

In order to reach these objectives, nurses are to have better access to funding, better career opportunities and better training. In addition, personnel development in general should be improved. One aspect of this is improved use of the skills, experience and knowledge of the nurses in their community and support for nurse practitioners. A new aspect is the support of nursing care by the government.

The government is very supportive of model projects to promote progress in the reorientation of nursing care. But the implementation of the model trials requires a fundamental cultural change on the part of the patients, other service providers, and the nurses themselves. There are particular difficulties when it comes to implementing projects in which the responsibilities of nurses are extended so that they overlap with those of other service providers.

Government support—skepticism from other stakeholders

There are no nationwide programs, regulations or guidelines for the development of nursing care in New Zealand. The projects originate at the local level and are directed to local needs. The projects are often initiated by nurses themselves or individual people or organizations. In part the projects are supported with funds from the Ministry of Health.

More local or regional initiatives

The model projects offer the opportunity to improve the quality and efficiency of nursing care. There are three central obstacles to implementation. The first is the inflexibility of work contracts. Second, the nursing care structures lack connections between the nurses providing basic care and intersectoral initiatives and public health services. A third key problem is training. Postgraduate programs are increasingly specialized, but for basic nursing care it is more important to provide a thoroughly based but broader spectrum of knowledge.

Expected results: improved quality and efficiency

Nurse practitioners are state qualified nurses who work as autonomous health practitioners with a defined spectrum of practical activities at a highly qualified practical level. By the end of 2005, the New Zealand government had extended the rights of nurse practitioners to prescribe drugs. Until then nurse practitioners had been entitled to write prescriptions for a limited range of drugs in the fields of "children and family health" and "caring for the elderly." With the amended legislation, the range of medications that the NPs can prescribe has been extended to

Increased responsibilities for nurse practitioners

more areas, including chronic conditions such as diabetes and cardiovascular diseases, and the promotion of health.

The extended rights of NPs to prescribe pharmaceutical products have been regulated by the government. The Nursing Council of New Zealand (NCNZ) has been put in charge of giving licences. In order to receive the prescription licence, NPs must satisfy defined preconditions: completion of an undergraduate course in nursing, a two-year clinical master's degree, a course in prescribing drugs at the master's level, at least four years nursing experience and the approval of the NCNZ for prescriptions. They must also provide evidence of their skills, take part in continuous training, apply for an annual practicing certificate, and accept an examination of their prescription activities by experts.

Promoting the employment of nurse practitioners
The assignment of nurse practitioners (NPs) is making only very slow progress in New Zealand. They were first introduced in 2000. By July 2006, only 25 nurse practitioners were actually working. A working party was set up in 2005 to examine the reasons for the low number. The remit of the working party was to identify barriers to a more rapid and comprehensive spread of NPs in New Zealand and to suggest how the role of NPs could be strengthened.

Recommendation on nurse practitioners
The Nurse Practitioner Employment and Development Working Party presented its first report to the ministry in May 2006. The recommendations were far-reaching and comprehensive. The health ministry then initiated a Nurse Practitioner Employment Facilitation Program aimed specifically at the District Health Boards. Details of the program's implementation were to be published.

Goals and recommendations of the working party
The basic goal of the working party was to accelerate the development of nurse practitioners in New Zealand. To achieve this goal, incentives should be provided to identify and create employment opportunities for NPs and appropriate training programs should be developed and recommended. In addition, the working party was to propose opportunities for financing and to examine possible partnerships and co-financing strategies with other service providers. Finally, they should identify nurse practitioner pathways that are aligned to the District Health Board and primary healthcare needs.

The working party recommended the facilitation of nurse practitioners so that highly qualified caring personnel would be able to coordinate the interface between hospital and community and offer a high level of medical services. Soon afterwards, further training programs were set up and requirements were formulated on the skills of nurse practitioners. For example, nurse practitioners will be entitled to prescribe a broad range of medications. The objective of the measures was to further develop the role of the nurse practitioner.

Whereas the nurses and the Ministry of Health were enthusiastic about the development of the role of the nurse practitioner, the medical profession expressed reservations. These related mainly to the rights of nurses to prescribe certain drugs.

Approval from nurses and government—but doctors have reservations

The details about how the Nurse Practitioner Employment Facilitation Program is to be implemented are still being worked out. The role of NPs will depend to a large extent on the active involvement of the potential employers, namely the District Health Boards, the Primary Health Organizations (PHOs) and some NGOs. PHOs are public, not-for-profit health institutions financed by flat-rate per capita charges, and they ensure the primary care of the people registered with them (see *Health Policy Developments*, issue 4, "Primary care for patients in need of special care"). Incentives and financial support will be needed to promote participation.

Further developments expected

An increase in the assignments of NPs could mean a fundamental change in the way health services in New Zealand are offered and organized. The number of experienced nurses who are enrolling for nurse practitioner training is rising rapidly. If the initiative to increase the availability of further training opportunities is effective, the role of NPs should be extended.

Experience from other countries shows that nurse practitioners play a key role in improving health. They reduce inequalities and the national burden of chronic disease and support the independent living of people with disabilities. The elimination of organizational barriers and the restructuring of traditional work structures are fundamental for the development of this role. In New Zealand, steps are being taken in this direction.

Sources and further reading:
CHSRP, University of Auckland. "Development of nurse practitioners." *Health Policy Monitor*, October 2006. www. hpm.org/survey/nz/a8/4.

CHSRP, Lisa Walton. "Nurse practitioner prescribing." *Health Policy Monitor*, April 2006. www.hpm.org/survey/ nz/a7/1.

CHSRP. "Models of primary health care nursing." *Health Policy Monitor*, April 2006. www.hpm.org/survey/nz/ a7/2.

Ministry of Health. Nurse Practitioners in New Zealand. Terms of Reference of the Nurse Practitioners Employment and Development Working Party. www.moh. govt.nz/moh.nsf/UnidPrint/MH4947?OpenDocument.

Ministry of Health. Nurse Practitioners in New Zealand. Wellington: Ministry of Health, 2002. www.moh.govt. nz/moh.nsf/fefd9e667cc713e9cc257011000678d8/16f47 058bbbc49d3cc256bf900721fa6/$FILE/NursePractitioners innz.pdf.

Ministry of Health. Evolving Models of Primary Health Care Nursing Practice. Wellington: Ministry of Health, 2005. www.moh.govt.nz/moh.nsf/0/7B8611D77164266 ECC25705B001BB6BA/$ File/EvolvNurse.pdf.

Ministry of Health. Investing in Health. A framework for activating primary health care nursing in New Zealand. Wellington: Ministry of Health, 2003. www.moh.govt. nz/moh.nsf/238fd5fb4fd051844c256669006aed57/a4d 86036478a63a7cc256bde006ff204/$FILE/InvestingIn Health.pdf.

Nursing Council New Zealand. "Nurse Practitioners." *New Zealand Gazette*, November 10, 2005.188. pp. 4750–4751. www.dia.govt.nz/pubforms.nsf/NZGZT/NZGazette188 Nov05.pdf/file/NZGazette188Nov05.pdf.

Japan: First work permits for Filipino nursing personnel

As part of the Economic Partnership Agreement (EPA) reached between Tokyo and Manila, Japan decided in September 2006 to allow Filipino nurses to work in the health service in Japan. The agreement with the Philippines is intended to help Japan cope with the imminent shortage of nursing personnel. It is the first time that people from abroad have been allowed to work in Japan.

The goal of the Japanese government is to ensure that there are sufficient numbers of personnel available to support its society, which is growing older and in which the numbers of births are declining. Japan has decided to accept up to 1,000 nurses and social workers from the Philippines over two years within the framework of the EPA. However, qualifications obtained in the Philippines are not necessarily recognized in Japan. Those with suitable qualifications will be able to stay in Japan for three years as "candidates." During this period they must obtain a regular work permit as a nurse. If they are not successful, they must return to the Philippines

Goals and content of the agreement

Communication between caring personnel from the Philippines and Japanese staff and patients will obviously be a problem. Therefore the nurses must demonstrate their language competence by passing a Japanese nursing exam in Japanese.

Overcoming language barriers

A Philippine nurse who starts out in Japan as a candidate will learn Japanese for six months and then work as a nursing assistant in hospitals and care institutions that have experience with trainee nurses. These hospitals and institutions must offer the Philippine personnel the same working conditions and wages as the Japanese employees. In addition, they must offer conditions which are conducive to learning Japanese. Whether the candidates finally succeed in obtaining the qualifications they will need to work as nurses in Japan will depend to a considerable extent on how seriously this obligation is taken by the various institutions.

Dire shortage of
nursing staff in
Japan calls for new
approaches

Many hospitals and other medical facilities in Japan are on the verge of a crisis because of the shortage of qualified nurses. Some experts estimate that as many as 40,000 nurses are needed. According to a study of the care for the elderly, fewer than 40 percent of care homes currently have enough personnel.

At the same time, no fewer than 8,000 nurses leave the Philippines every year to work in Saudi Arabia, continental Europe, and the Americas. The caring personnel have an excellent reputation for their skills and knowledge. English is spoken in most of the countries in which the nurses can work, so that the language barriers are minimal.

On September 8, 2006, the Philippines and Japan reached a bilateral free trade agreement, the Japan-Philippines Economic Partnership Agreement (JPEPA). It will open up a new dimension in the Philippine-Japanese trade relationships.

The Association of Household Helpers fears that Filipinos will be employed as cheap labor and that working conditions will become worse for all caring personnel. The Japanese Trade Union for Medical Personnel sees a long-term risk that Japan, like England, will lose its capacity to train its own medical personnel if qualified nurses are employed from other countries.

The Japanese Nursing Association, in contrast, argues that it is important to make up for the shortage of domestic personnel, provided that employment opportunities for Japanese nurses are guaranteed.

In the Philippines, the knowledge of Japanese is seen as a very demanding requirement. In the opinion of the Philippine Association of Nurses, this makes it much more difficult to meet the Japanese nursing requirements.

According to a recommendation of the Manila-based Asian Institutes of Management Policy, Japan could ease these requirements by allowing non-Japanese-speaking nursing personnel to care for English-speaking Japanese. Because this group would mostly belong to the higher strata of society, they would often be able to employ private nursing personnel.

Because the required knowledge of Japanese will probably be the greatest barrier for the Filipino nurses and carers, it is expected that they will not be able to make full use of the opportunities offered by the bilateral agreement with Japan.

Sources and further reading:
Sato, Masayo. "Acceptance of nurses from the Philippines."
Health Policy Monitor, October 2006. www.hpm.org/
survey/jp/a8/1.

Canada: Pan-Canadian planning to counter personnel shortages

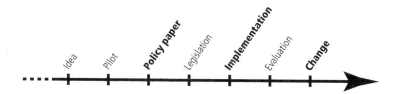

In December 2005, the governments of the 13 provinces and territories in Canada wanted to present detailed plans for the future development of personnel in the health system. They had reached this joint decision in a 10-year plan for the improvement of public health care in the previous year. A reorientation was very important, because Canada has been suffering from an acute shortage of medical personnel. Two sector studies on the distribution of doctors showed that in view of these shortages of personnel, Canada would have to regulate the training and distribution at the national level; it would no longer be able to delegate this responsibility to the provinces and territories. In addition to the reassessment of the numbers of personnel required, the provinces and territories are called on to create new definitions for cross-sectoral vocations, so that medical personnel would be given new roles (e.g., academically trained nurses and midwives) and could be deployed more flexibly.

In the past, medical personnel in Canada were trained in depth to prepare for work in a special field. The numbers required would be calculated on the basis of model predictions of requirements. At the start of the 1990s, the predictions indicated that there would be an oversupply of doctors for the provinces and territories in the coming decade. The consequence was a drastic

Shortage of doctors and ...

161

reduction in the numbers admitted to higher education institutions to study medicine. As it turned out, the predictions were wrong. In many regions there is already a shortage of doctors, in particular of general practitioners. The results are long waiting lists for treatment. Patients from remote areas often have to travel long distances for medical care.

In recent years, the provinces and territories have attempted to make good the shortages by recruiting doctors from other countries (mainly from Asia and Africa). However, national and international pressure has persuaded the provinces and territories to terminate this strategy, which had questionable implications for development policies.

... poor conditions for nursing personnel

Canada also finds itself facing considerable problems when it comes to nursing personnel. Sufficient numbers are being trained, but the heavy workloads and poor pay mean that many only work part-time and take up additional, less demanding jobs. Many nursing personnel quit long before reaching the official retirement age.

Competition among provinces and territories

The notorious shortage of doctors has in the past led to financial wrangling among the 13 provinces and territories. The richer ones have been offering financial incentives to lure doctors from other regions. But that has only exacerbated the shortages of doctors in the less wealthy parts of the country, such as the Yukon Territory.

Results so far uneven

By December 2005, eight of the 13 provincial and territorial governments had presented plans to improve the personnel situation. The province of Saskatchewan was the only one to engage in public discussions with the main stakeholders to define future goals and possible strategies for the implementation. The other provinces and territories have only partly consulted affected groups such as the associations of doctors and of nurses. There is still an absence of specific proposals on how to reach the goals. There is widespread approval at the national level for reorganizing the training of doctors and nursing personnel, but the provinces and territories are worried that in the future they may have less control.

Experts are predicting that national measures and legislation are only necessary to establish new occupational groups. The 13 health ministries will take on the task of implementing the national decisions at the regional level. Quality improvements through improved access and shorter waiting times will lead in the coming years to a stabilization of the Canadian health system.

Sources and further reading:
McIntosh, Tom. "Provincial Health Human Resource Plans." *Health Policy Monitor,* April 2006. www.hpm. org/survey/ca/a7/2.

Health Canada. Pan-Canadian Health Human Resources Planning. www.hcsc.gc.ca/hcssss/hhr-rhs/strateg/plan/ index_e.html.
Health Council of Canada. Progress Update. Wait Times and Health Human Resources. Health Care Renewal in Canada. Annual Report to Canadians, 2005. Ottawa: Health Council of Canada, 2006.
McIntosh, Tom, and Renee Torgerson. *Setting Priorities and Getting Direction. Conference Report.* Ottawa: Canadian Policy Research Networks, 2006.

France: Plan for demographic development of doctors

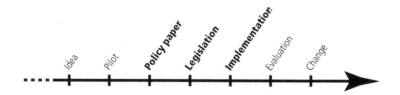

In January 2006, the French government issued a national plan on the future development of medical personnel. The background for this measure is presented by the extreme differences in care between urban and rural areas, an imminent shortage of doctors and the need to improve the quality of care. The plan rests on three pillars and will change the future development of medical personnel.

First, the disparity between rural and urban regions has to be redressed. A region will be classified as remote if the density of doctors there is 30 percent below the average. To attract more doc-

Public visibility

Impact

Transferability

Redressing regional differences

163

tors to such regions in the future, the plan proposes three financial incentives. The sickness funds should pay 20 percent more in rural regions for each treatment. Furthermore, local authorities will have the possibility of providing financial support to doctors wishing to establish a new surgery or to provide them with free accommodations. Authorities can offer students grants of up to 24,000 euros or make accommodations available to them if they undertake to work in the region for at least five years after qualifying. The third financial incentive is directed at doctors who provide 24-hour service. They will be rewarded with a tax rebate of up to 9,000 euros per year on their income.

Working together, not alone

The second pillar of the plan envisages a substantial improvement in working conditions for doctors. In the future, doctors should be able to cooperate in group practice, which should considerably improve their working conditions and the quality of care. Young doctors can work as partners of general practitioners without having to invest their own capital. The final aspect of the second pillar is aimed at offering as much maternal leave for women doctors as for women in all the other sectors of the French economy. Previously this period had been shorter.

Revising former miscalculations: more doctors (again)

The third pillar of the plans involves an increase in the numbers of medical students. This has become necessary as a result of the introduction of the 35-hour week in hospitals and the need to replace a wave of French doctors now approaching retirement age. Since 2006, an additional 700 places have been made available for students, so that the number starting to study medicine has increased to 7,000 per year. In addition, since 2006 medical students have been required to train for two months with a general practitioner. This is intended to provide an incentive and attract more students to this profession. In 2005, there was a shortfall of 600 applicants for courses in general medicine.

Finally, more doctors in France should work until the official retirement age of 65. To encourage this, the cap on additional income (on top of pensions) will be increased from 30,000 to 40,000 euros for doctors retiring later than at 65. Furthermore on reaching the age of 60, they will no longer have to be available around the clock.

Plan involves interest groups

Many of the changes proposed in the strategy paper were developed by the ONDPS (Observatoire National de la Démographie des Professions de Santé), which was set up by the health ministry to examine the demographic development of medical personnel. The commission took care to formulate the proposals in consensus with the various interest groups. Initially, the commission intended to develop a requirement plan that determined the maximum number of doctors in each special field for each region. However, the representatives of the medical students were not in agreement. A compromise was reached for a 20-percent increase in payments for doctors in remote regions. However, in principle it seems that the representatives of the interest groups now accept the plan. So far no evaluation is planned, but ONDPS will continue to observe the trends and developments in the medical profession.

Sources and further reading:
Bourgueil, Yann, and Karine Chevreul. "Demographic plan for health professionals." *Health Policy Monitor,* 14/04/2006. www.hpm.org/survey/fr/a7/1.

Ministère de la Santé et des Solidarités. Response au Défi de la Démographie Médicale. www.sante.gouv.fr/htm/ dossiers/demographie_medicale/sommaire.htm.

Australia: Reforms to reverse past mistakes

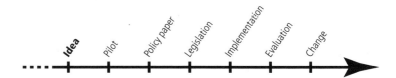

Idea — Pilot — Policy paper — Legislation — Implementation — Evaluation — Change

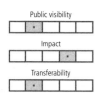

Public visibility

Impact

Transferability

**Ten-year plan
to make up for
unforeseen
developments**

**Poor access due
to shortages of
personnel**

**More mobility for
qualified personnel**

In January 2006, a government commission presented a report outlining reform options for the development of medical personnel in Australia. The background of the report is an acute shortage of trained personnel in the health services and bureaucratic barriers to the recognition of qualifications.

The goal of the government is to develop a reform plan for the coming 10 years on the basis of the reform proposals. The aim is to redress the unforeseen consequences of past personnel policies. The report also refers mainly to the future development of supply, the acceptance of qualifications, and the distribution of medical personnel. The report places particular emphasis on the increase in the numbers of people admitted for training and on improvements in the quality of training provided.

Already today there is a shortfall of about 10,000 nurses and 1,200 general practitioners in Australia. An additional shortage of specialists is also predicted for the coming years. This situation is a consequence of cuts in the numbers admitted for training as nurses and doctors in the 1980s and 1990s, when the government expected that there would be an oversupply of medical personnel. The shortages have already been having a negative influence on the access to health care for some years. There are now waiting lists for certain procedures and treatments. For some parts of the population, the supposedly free access to the system is further impeded by the rising co-payments.

A central point is to improve the mobility and flexibility of qualified personnel. A national register is proposed to replace the previous state registration of medical personnel. In the past, qualified personnel could work in another federal state only if they were first registered there, which meant contacting the relevant regional authorities and paying new registration fees. In practice, these bureaucratic barriers gave regions with acute shortages little chance of recruiting personnel from other parts of the country.

Another recommendation in the report is that the Australian health insurance, Medicare, be opened up to other providers of care, such as midwives, who had previously been excluded from public funding. Lobby groups for these care providers have long called for the removal of the barriers that reserve privileges to special professional groups. However, the government is worried that it would become more difficult to control expenditures. An increase in competition could in part break up monopolies.

Opening Medicare for other providers of care

Overall, the report provided few specific proposals about matters relating to financing, such as how unequal financial incentives could be removed. For example, it is unclear whether providers of care such as midwives and podiatrists should be paid on the basis of lists of services, with flat fees, or in some other way.

At a meeting of state health ministers and the national government in April 2006, the first signs of the reforms began to crystallize. By June 2007, legal alterations were to be put in place for the national accreditation of medical personnel. Furthermore, the government in Canberra has decided to finance selected forms of psychotherapy through Medicare and thus open up the market for other care providers. So far there have been no indications from the government about increases in the numbers of admissions to medical courses to counter the threat of shortages of personnel in the future.

First reactions unstructured

Sources and further reading:
van Gool, Kees. "Options for Health Workforce Reform in Australia." *Health Policy Monitor*, April 2006. www.hpm. org/survey/au/a7/1.

Australian Government Productivity Commission. Australia's Health Workforce. Productivity Commission Research Report. Canberra: Productivity Commission, 2005. www.pc.gov.au/study/healthworkforce/finalreport/healthworkforce.pdf.

Slovenia: Struggle with a shortage of nurses

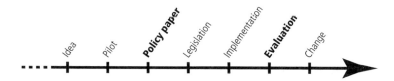

Public visibility

Impact

Transferability

Slovenia has assessed its need for nurses for the coming 25 years, and the results show that at the end of 2005 there was a deficit in 12 counties of around 300 personnel needed for the care of patients. With only 1.95 million people living in Slovenia, this figure is high. Even though the number of training places has increased in recent years, it will only be possible to make up for the shortages gradually because the duration of training has been increased to improve the quality of care.

Predictions of shortages
It is predicted for the coming 25 years that there will be a continued shortage—with about 1,000 nurses lacking. Four factors were mentioned in the report of the health ministry as causes of the current and future shortage of nurses. First, the number of (long-term) patients in Slovenia is increasing as its population ages. Second, in the coming years many nurses will be reaching retirement age and will have to be replaced. Third, the transfer of medical responsibilities from the doctor to nurses to cut costs is increasing demands. Fourth, the future limitation of working hours within the European Union will also have an impact on the working capacity of the nursing personnel. Nurses currently have a very heavy workload. A reduction in working hours will have to be met by recruiting more nursing staff.

Brain gain is no alternative
Recruiting nurses from other countries is no alternative for Slovenia, because other EU member states are themselves struggling with shortages of personnel. Some health institutions have already been unsuccessful in their attempts to recruit personnel, in particular doctors, from neighboring countries.

National strategy needed
The report at hand has made clear that the government will have to undertake measures to counter shortages of nursing personnel. The representatives of the interested groups in the Slovenian health system are in agreement about this. Another increase in training opportunities is unavoidable. At the same time

it will be important to keep a close track on developments in the coming years to prevent the increase in the number of trainees leading to more trained nurses than are required over the long term, so that some will later be faced with unemployment.

Sources and further reading:
Albreht, Tit. "Nursing professional demography—projections." *Health Policy Monitor*, April 2006. www.hpm. org/survey/si/a7/2.

Institute of Public Health of the Republic of Slovenia. Analysis of the needs for nurses with projections for the needs until 2032. Ljubljana, 2005.

England and Wales: New funding system for dental treatment

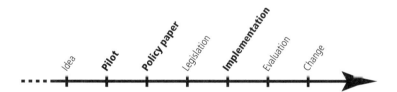

In April 2006, England and Wales introduced a new funding system for NHS dental treatment. The previous system, with more than 400 listed benefits, has been replaced by three groups of benefits. At the same time, to make dental care more accessible the maximum co-payment of the patients has been more than halved from £ 384 to £ 189.

The British government refers to the changes as the greatest reform in dental care since 1948. It has been working on the restructuring of the payments for dental treatment since the end of the 1990s, because evaluations showed that these were inefficient and unfair. In contrast to many other countries, dental treatment in England and Wales is a fixed element of the publicly funded benefit basket.

Dental services are financed through 302 local primary care trusts. Since 2005, these have already been receiving the entire NHS dental care budget. Within the three new payment groups, the dentists will now receive £15 for prophylactic measures, £41 for simple treatment (fillings, etc.) and £183 for complicated dental procedures (crowns, bridges, etc.). This division is intended to eliminate any incentive dentists may feel to carry out unnecessary procedures to improve their income. The expected effect is that dentists will have more time in the future for their patients because they will only be doing the necessary work. At the same time, the health ministry expects considerable savings for the dentists, because the flat-rate payments will cut the administrative work.

Under the old payment arrangements, dentists were dissatisfied because the level of income was very volatile, and this was a reason why some dentists left the NHS. The new payment system guarantees dentists a minimum annual income of £80,000, after deduction of surgery costs, until mid-2009. Furthermore, the dentists will be able to participate in the NHS pension program. On the basis of the ensured income, the government and the dentists have agreed to a reduction of 5 percent in the dentists' treatment volume. The time gained is to be used for preventive measures.

Pilot projects, in which about 30 percent of all NHS dentists participated, show that the treatment volume declined overall by 30 percent. This result came about because dentists in the old system induced additional demand and thus were maximizing revenues.

The reduction of the co-payments for expensive treatment can improve access for some patients and thus increase the fairness of the system. Furthermore, cream-skimming can be avoided. For example, in the past some dentists would only accept children as NHS patients if their parents were registered as private patients.

So far, all parties are welcoming the reforms introduced by the government. However, the full effects of the new payment system are still unclear. The government has therefore brought together a group of stakeholder representatives (consumer associations, consumer advice centers, the dental association, etc.) to monitor implementation and evaluate the results. In particular, their remit includes examining whether the standardized financial measures have resulted in dentists only carrying out necessary measures.

Sources and further reading:
Oliver, Adam. "Implementing the NHS dental reforms." *Health Policy Monitor,* April 2006. Implementing the NHS dental reforms. www.hpm.org/survey/uk/a7/5.

Department of Health. Implementation group invited to give dental reforms regular check up. London, 2006.
Department of Health. Modernising NHS Dentistry. Implementing the NHS Plan. London: Department of Health, 2000. www.dh.gov.uk/assetRoot/04/01/93/04/04019304.pdf.
Oliver, Adam. Reforming public sector dentistry in the UK. *British Journal of Health Care Management* (8): 212–216, 2000.
Robinson, Ray. The economics of dental care. *Euro Observer* (6) 2: 4–6, 2004. www.euro.who.int/document/Obs/EuroObserver6_2.pdf.

Singapore: Outsourcing x-ray analysis to India

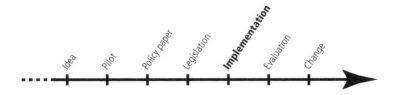

Since December 2005, under a commercial agreement with India's Teleradiology Solutions, one of Singapore's polyclinics has been sending about 700 x-rays a month—or about 30 a day—to India for analysis and reporting. From April 2006, the Indian radiologists will take over the reading of simple x-rays from more polyclinics, and eventually from all nine polyclinics under the National Healthcare Group.

171

Cost effective ... Some doctors have protested against this outsourcing of the analysis of x-ray images to India, arguing that it is not cheaper to have x-rays analyzed abroad. The health ministry countered that the analysis of an image in Singapore costs more than SGD 30, whereas in the Indian polyclinic the costs were considerably lower. Another advantage of the international cooperation is that patients in Singapore no longer have to wait an average of two weeks for the results of their x-rays but can receive them the same day. That means that patients are spared a second visit to the polyclinic and another consultation fee.

... with high quality Singapore's College of Radiologists, as the MoH-appointed accreditation body, made site visits at the institute in Bangalore and declared that the standards there were appropriate. In addition, the provider was accredited by America's Joint Comission on Accreditation of Health Care Organizations.

Following America's example In its decision to have x-rays analyzed in other countries, Singapore has followed the example of the United States. For some years, U.S. hospitals have been sending x-rays for night-time emergency cases to the same company in Bangalore. Within 30 minutes, they receive a complete analysis from India. The 20 radiologists of the Indian radiological institute process some 500 images every day from more than 50 U.S. hospitals—from common x-ray to 64-layer computed tomography. The institute is reported to have an enviable track record of 99.8 percent accuracy in its diagnosis, exceeding the US requirement of 96 percent accuracy.

Trend continues The Ministry of Health in Singapore has announced that in the future it will carry out more double-blind checks on the evaluation of x-ray images in Singapore and in other countries in order to maintain the quality of the investigations at the highest level. The ministry is also encouraging the development of teleradiology infrastructure in Singapore, which is in line with its vision of positioning Singapore as a major center providing high-end and complex imaging services to other countries, in addition to Singapore. With the developments of information and communications technology, globalization has begun to achieve successes in the field of health care.

172

Sources and further reading:
Department of Community, Occupational & Family Medicine, National University of Singapore. "Singapore outsources X-rays to Bangalore." *Health Policy Monitor,* April 2006. www.hpm.org/survey/sg/a7/1.

Drug policies and pricing

In most OECD countries, more than three-quarters of all expenditures for drugs are provided through public systems. Physicians and patients scarcely react to changes in the prices of pharmaceutical products because costs are almost totally covered by health insurance. In many industrialized countries, pharmaceutical expenditures have been increasing over the past decade by an average of 6 percent per year and now account for 14.6 percent of health service expenditures (OECD, 2005).

The failure of the market is forcing the political regulation of **Market failure in** the market for pharmaceutical products. But this involves taking **the drugs sector** into consideration the interests and positions of the providers of funds, the consumers and the producers (see fig. 3). The profit-oriented pharmaceutical sector has strong lobbies in countries such as the United States, France, Great Britain, Japan and Germany, and they attempt to exert political influence on the certification of their products and their market share, as well as on payments by the publicly funded health service. For their part, payers—whether health insurance funds or national health services—want to keep the expenditure on drugs as low as possible, or at least to get the most quantity and quality for "their" money. Consumers—both the patients and the prescribing doctors—expect that politicians will secure a comprehensive supply of pharmaceutical products as part of universal health insurance coverage, with the patients wishing also to keep supplementary payments as low as possible. In the following, some mechanisms are described that have been developed and tested in other countries to regulate the pharmaceutical market and to minimize cost increases.

Decisions about which drugs to include in the benefit basket not only regulate the entitlements of those insured (and for Ameri-

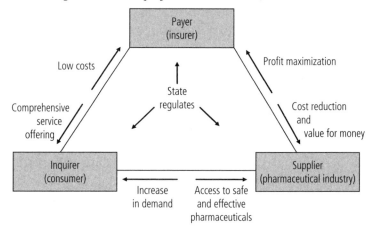

Source: Authors' own compilation

Regulation by limitation of the benefits catalogue

cans over the age of 65, these now also include drugs; see page 179) but can also influence the costs of pharmaceutical products. Each country has its own rules determining which items are eligible for inclusion in the catalogue. The decision can be based on the therapeutic benefit of a drug and on economic considerations. Many countries are determining the additional benefit offered by a product and assessing this against the additional cost. It is also possible to view this the other way around: The additional benefit offered by a new drug over the established one can put a limit on its price.

Price determination reduces costs

A second instrument in national pricing policies is to fix the reimbursement rates for drugs in the benefit basket. A country establishes prices that do not threaten the financing system but that are economical for the pharmaceutical companies. There are two common approaches to the determination of price. In one, the prices are fixed directly. Frequently adopted for patent-protected drugs, this method has been used in all EU-15 member states except Germany and Great Britain. There are various approaches. In addition to linking the price to the additional benefit, as mentioned above, some countries also refer to the average or maximum price paid in a group of other countries.

Reference price systems are the second form of price determination. These are widely used instruments aimed at establishing the maximum amount paid for groups of drugs with the same active substances, with comparable pharmacological substances, or with comparable therapeutic effects. Generally, the application of a fixed-sum system can contribute to reducing costs.

Spain is now also introducing a reference price system for patent-protected drugs, after the costs for pharmaceutical products increased by 11 percent in 2003 (see page 182). The inclusion of all patent-protected drugs could lead to cost reductions because the manufacturers have been able to set their own prices for patent-protected pharmaceutical products, which are not covered by the price regulations. In addition to positive lists, Poland is also introducing a three-tier reimbursement system (see page 185). **Fixed sums for patent-protected drugs**

In the past, the promotion of generic products after the expiration of patent coverage for the original product has proved to be an important instrument for reducing the annual increase in costs for pharmaceutical products. Many publicly funded health systems have taken the prices for generic products as their point of orientation in the calculations for their fixed-sum systems. In the United States, private health insurers began offering a reduced premium in 2006 for Medicare drug insurance if the policy holder agrees to receive a generic substitution (see page 179). **Substituting generics for original products**

Another approach to damping the costs for pharmaceutical products is to increase control over the way doctors issue prescriptions. The use of electronic prescription systems simplifies this measure and should encourage doctors to pay greater attention to the way they prescribe drugs. The Spanish region of Catalonia has launched a pilot project for the electronic prescription of drugs (see page 187). **More control over prescribing behavior**

In the past, bureaucratic obstacles and questions of safety have limited the introduction of innovative monitoring methods. New legislation is also being introduced in the United States to introduce technological innovations for prescribing medicine (see page 187).

Another way to influence the quality and consumption of pharmaceutical products and their supplies is to introduce legislation regulating public advertising of prescription drugs. New Zealand and the United States are currently the only countries **Restricting advertising for drugs** with unlimited freedom of advertising for pharmaceutical companies. In New Zealand, a gap in legislation is responsible for this situation, and the government intends to close the gap to protect consumers against misleading advertising (see page 191).

Sources and further reading:
Danzon, Patricia M., and Jonathan D. Katcham. *Reference pricing of pharmaceuticals for medicare. Evidence from Germany, the Netherlands, and New Zealand.* Working Paper 10007, National Bureau of Economic Research. New York, 2003.
European Federation of Pharmaceutical Industries and Associations. The pharmaceutical industry in figures 2006. www.efpia.org/Objects/2/Files/infigures2006.pdf.
Freemantle, Nick, and Suzanne Hill. *Evaluating Pharmaceuticals for Health Policy and Reimbursement.* Oxford: Blackwell BMJ Books, 2004.
Jacobzone, Stéphane. *Pharmaceutical Policies in OECD Countries: Reconciling social and industrial goals.* Paris: OECD, 2000.
López Casasnovas, Guillem, and Bengt Jönsson (eds.): *Reference pricing and pharmaceutical policy.* Barcelona: Springer Iberica, 2001.
Mossialos, Elias, Monique Mrazek and Tom Walley. *Regulating pharmaceuticals in Europe: Striving for efficiency, equity and quality.* Maidenhead: Open University Press, 2004.
OECD. Health Data 2005. www.oecd.org/document/44/0,2340,en_2649_34631_2085228_1_1_1_1,00.html.

United States: Medicare Part D introduced

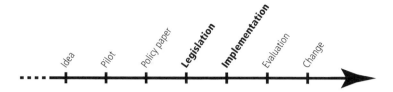

Since January 2006 Medicare participants have been able to take out coverage against unacceptable costs for prescription drugs. Seniors (persons 65 and older) and people with disabilities had previously been insured only for stationary treatment (Medicare Part A) and outpatient treatment (Medicare Part B). Medicare Part C covers the same benefits as Part A and Part B, but insurees' choice of physicians is restricted. For example, Medicare Part C participants have to choose their doctors from a predefined list of providers or from a provider network. With Medicare Part D, participants can now take out coverage for medication costs with private insurance companies certified by Medicare. These companies offer individual premium models based on the standard package specified by the legislation.

Participants pay an average monthly premium of USD 37 (about 28 euros) and have to pay the first $250 (186 euros) for medication every year themselves. After that, the personal contribution depends on the insurance plan chosen. With the standard plan, participants pay 25 percent of the costs, up to $2,250 (1,675 euros). After this threshold, they have to meet all the costs up to a limit of $5,100 (3,797 euros). After spending $3,600 (2,680 euros) out of pocket for medication, they only have to contribute 5 percent for further medication within the current year (see figure 4). This limitation is intended to protect people with extremely high drug needs and costs from catastrophic expenditures. If participants cannot pay for the costs, they can apply for these to be covered by Medicare.

The doughnut hole insurance

This new legislation is to lead to savings and long-term reductions in the costs for supplying medications. Premium models of the insurance companies provide incentives to prescribe generic drugs. Participants can pay less for their insurance if they accept generic medicines rather than branded products. If any side

Savings expected on medication costs

179

Fig. 4: The Medicare doughnut hole

Cost share

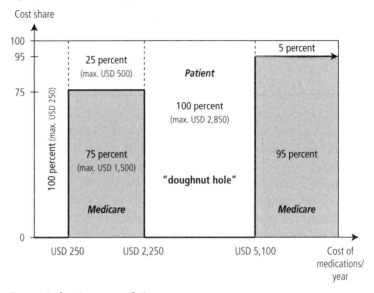

Source: Authors' own compilation

effects are caused by the generic medicine, then the original product can be prescribed in a second step. The insurance companies
can also require the doctor to obtain approval before prescribing
specific groups of medicines ("prior authorization"). Another method used to reduce costs is the limitation of the quantities prescribed. A patient who has to take one tablet a day for 30 days will
be given exactly 30 tablets.

Law aims at rapid   It has been possible for patients to sign up for the medication
introduction insurance since mid-November 2005. The law envisaged a surcharge of 1 percent for each month of delay for applications submitted after May 15, 2006. The aim of this provision was to promote the rapid and widespread introduction of the insurance. By
the end of March 2006, some 27 million Medicare participants
had already decided in favor of Medicare Part D, and by the start
of November 2006 the number had risen to 32.8 million. This
meant that the government had more than met its target of enrolling 28 million to 30 million participants within the first year for
the new Medicare medication insurance.

180

The large numbers of people signing up in the first months is an indication of the importance they attach to insurance against high medication costs with Medicare Part D. President Bush positively appraised the introduction phase of Medicare Part D despite the initial difficulties with the distribution of funds. Competition among the providers, according to Bush, had already led to lower premiums. On average, participants were paying only half as much for pharmaceutical products as they had been paying before. There were also clear signs of cost reductions due to the incentive to prescribe generic medicines. Government satisfied so far

In the opinion of the opposition Democrats, however, the legislation needed improvements. They argued that the three-month deadline for the applications was too short. Medicare participants should first have had the opportunity to thoroughly compare the prices and the packages offered by the insurance companies. The variety of the insurance policies on offer made comparison even more difficult. Democrats also thought that a premium surcharge of 1 percent for each month of delay was too high. Without adequate time to take out an insurance policy, the participants would be unable to avoid making the wrong choices. Senator Hillary Clinton announced that she was working on an improved draft of the bill. Resistance from the ranks of the opposition …

Calls for improvements were voiced by the American Psychological Association, the Epilepsy Association and representatives of people with disabilities. They also demanded that rapid reimbursements be made to participants who because of miscalculations had had to pay too much out of their own pockets. Pharmacists were also waiting for their money after calculation errors. AARP, the largest association for persons 50 and older and representing more than 35 million members, welcomed the new insurance in principle. The association expects the law to lead to cost reductions in the provision of medicines. … and from interest groups

It is not yet clear what level of cost reductions will be achieved by Medicare Part D or how it will ease the burden on individuals and in particular on the socially disadvantaged. The short introductory period did not provide a basis for estimates. However, it is important that the first effects of Medicare Part D be investigated early so that any imbalances may be corrected. Evaluation necessary

181

Sources and further reading:

Huynh, Phuong Trang and Stuart Guterman. "US Medicare Prescription Drug Coverage." *Health Policy Monitor,* April 2006. www.hpm.org/survey/us/b7/3.

Hoadley, Jack. Medicare's New Adventure: The Part D Drug Benefit. The Commonwealth Fund, March 2006. www.cmwf.org/publications/publications_show.htm? doc_id=362249.

Smith, Vernon, Kathleen Gifford and Sandy Kramer. Observations on the initial implementation of the Medicare Prescription Drug Program, May 2006. www.kff. org/medicaid/ upload/7520.pdf.

Stuart, Bruce, Becky A. Briesacher, Dennis G. Shea and Barbara S. Cooper. Riding the Rollercoaster: The Ups and Downs in Out-of-Pocket Spending Under the Standard Medicare Drug Benefit. *Health Affairs* 24(4): 1022–1031, 2005.

U.S. Department of Health and Human Services. Medicare. www.medicare.gov/default.asp.

Spain: Draft legislation to rationalize the use of pharmaceuticals

Public visibility

Impact

Transferability

With the goal of achieving a long-term reduction in the high expenditure on pharmaceutical products, the Spanish Ministry of Health presented a bill to parliament in December 2005 on rationalization of the use of medicines which was passed in summer 2006. In 2005, almost a quarter of all funding in the health system was spent on pharmaceutical products, with a growth of 5.7 percent over 2004. In the EU-15 member states, only Portugal has

182

been spending a similarly large proportion of its health budget on pharmaceutical products; in Germany, the proportion is about 10 percentage points lower.

Already in 2007, the ministry aims to save 1 billion euros, about 10 percent of the expenditure on drugs. The draft legislation is based on a strategy paper of the health ministry published at the end of 2004 (see report in *Health Policy Developments,* issue 5).

In addition to a reference price system for nonpatented medications, a reference price system for patented medications replaces the former price calculation for patent-protected pharmaceutical products. The arithmetic mean costs of the three least expensive products in a group of drugs are used as the maximum payment sum. A group must include at least one generic product. In addition, the law implements for a 20 percent price rebate on all medications that have been on the market for more than 10 years.

Reference prices based on the three least expensive products

The law also envisages selective funding of medications. In the future, drugs will be paid in accordance with their therapeutic benefit. An interdisciplinary commission (CIP) will be responsible for assessing the therapeutic benefit. The commission will draw on the evaluations provided by the Spanish Agency for Pharmaceutical and Health Products (AEMPS).

A special clause is intended to stimulate increased use of generics over original products. Generics should receive market approval immediately after patent protection for the original medication expires. Producers of generic drugs can use their own product names (instead of just the name of the active substance) to promote the marketing of the generic.

More generics, more advertising

In the future, Spanish pharmaceutical companies will have to make periodic payments to the public health system. The level of these contributions depends on the annual turnover of the company. The revenues generated are used for funding research projects and for the training of specialized staff. Manufacturers can reduce their payment by up to 35 percent if they take part in Profarma, the public program supporting innovations in the pharmaceutical sector.

Pharmaceutical companies sponsor public research

Furthermore, in the future drug companies will not be allowed to offer rebates to pharmacies for bulk orders or to distribute advertising presents to doctors. In addition, the sale of pharmaceutical products through the Internet is to be prohibited.

Fearing considerable financial losses, pharmaceutical companies and wholesalers are vehemently resisting the law. They are attempting to exert pressure on politicians, arguing that the reform in the drugs sector would reduce the investment volume of manufacturers and thus lead to a substantial loss of jobs. In some of the autonomous regions of Spain, the pharmaceutical industry makes a considerable contribution to the gross domestic product; some regional parliaments, such as Madrid, have come out against the legislation.

Nevertheless, the Spanish parliament was not intimidated by these threats. A long-term easing of the financial burden on the health system and a reduction in the profits of the pharmaceutical industry are essential. At the end of 2007, it will be possible to see what savings have been achieved through the law.

Sources and further reading:
Sánchez, Elvira. "Rationalizing use of drugs and health products." *Health Policy Monitor,* April 2006. www.hpm. org/survey/es/a7/3.

Costa-Font, Joan and Jaume Puig-Junoy. *Regulatory ambivalence and the limitations of pharmaceutical policy in Spain.* Working Paper Ref. 762, June 2004. Department of Economics and Business, Universitat Pompeu Fabra.
Ministerio de Sanidad y Consumo. Dirección General de Farmacia y Productos Sanitarios. www.msc.es/en/profe sionales/farmacia/organizacion.htm.
Puig-Junoy, Jaume. *The Impact of Generic Reference Pricing Interventions in the Statin Market.* Working Paper Ref. 762, December 2005. Department of Economics and Business, Universitat Pompeu Fabra.

Poland: More transparency in drug reimbursements

After the parliamentary election of September 2005, the Polish government decided to reform the reimbursement system for pharmaceutical products. To this end, the health ministry presented various reform approaches in a strategy paper on the approval and reimbursement of drugs. In the past there had been no rational system in Poland for the reimbursement for pharmaceutical products. Therefore, the costs of urgently needed drugs were frequently not reimbursed, in particular for new, innovative, and therefore often expensive products. By contrast, the national health insurance service paid in full for older, less expensive products.

The law on pharmaceutical products passed in 2001 had the goal of introducing transparency into the remuneration system for drugs in accordance with European Directive 89/105. However, this act was found ineffectual when it came to its practical implementation. Service providers, patients, and experts blamed the extremely high drug expenses on the continuing lack of transparency and errors in decision-making in the intersectoral drug-management committee. That committee was made up of representatives of the ministries of health, finance, economics, and social affairs and the national health insurance organization.

The health ministry's strategy paper concentrated on the rationalization of the reimbursement mechanisms for pharmaceutical products. According to the paper, the current intersectoral medicines committee is to be dissolved and replaced by a special commission. This commission is to set up two positive lists, one for medicines taken frequently and one for drugs administered infrequently. Both lists are to be updated annually, and every medicine should be resubmitted for registration every five years. The introduction of drugs in accordance with the standards of the European Medicines Agency (EMEA) is expected to

A maze of remunerations

lead to rapid but secure access to medication. At the same time, the drugs must also fit in with the national list of priorities and the financial resources of the national health insurance system.

Eight-point plan for drug reimbursements In addition, medicines in the future would be assigned to the classes "generics" or "innovative products." A generic drug would be reimbursed through the national health insurance system only if it has passed a bioequivalence test and is at least 30 percent less expensive than the original product. Overall, three criteria would determine eligibility: price, effectiveness, and therapy indications. The only exception would be medicines whose clinical benefit is not much lower than that of previous products but which are considerably less expensive.

The strategy paper proposes three reimbursement levels for pharmaceutical products: a reference price, 30 percent of costs, or 50 percent of costs. The reference price would be defined on the basis of the defined daily dose. The previous full reimbursement would no longer be provided.

As a final point, the strategy paper proposes two options for price formation and profit margins. The first option is the introduction of official fixed prices and official profit margins for wholesalers and pharmacies. The second option proposes maximum retail prices and fixed margins for wholesalers. The profits of pharmacists for the products in question would also be limited. It was not clear which of these two options would be preferred.

Controversial positions... Whereas patients and doctors have welcomed the proposed changes to the legislation, the pharmaceutical companies fear that some of their drugs might not be included in the new list. Therefore, they oppose changes in the rebates for prescribed medicines. Experts are worried that pharmaceutical companies could also exert leverage on the future legislation through corruption.

... impeding the legislative process To ensure that patients will be reimbursed through the health insurance system for the medicines they really need, there is an urgent need to introduce new legislation. The various possible forms of regulation are demonstrated by the strategy paper, but these are disputed. Government representatives must decide on a joint approach to ensure successful completion of the project to overcome the lack of transparency in the Polish system of remuneration for medicines.

Sources and further reading:
Mokrzycka, Anna and Iwona Kowalska. "Ideas of drugs reimbursement system changes." *Health Policy Monitor,* April 2006. www.hpm.org/survey/pl/a7/1.

National Health Fund. *Access to health care during a temporary stay in Poland.* www.nfz.gov.pl/ue/index.php?katnr= 5&dzialnr=2&artnr=716&czartnr=2.
Pharmaceutical Inspectorate. Organisational scheme of pharmaceutical inspection. www.gif.gov.pl/en_soi_schema. html.
European Medicines Agency. www.emea.eu.int/.

Spain and the United States: Electronic prescriptions

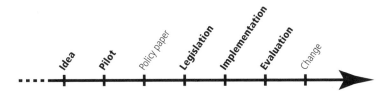

Spain and the United States want to increase the use of electronic prescription of drugs. While the widespread implementation of "e-prescribing" faces legislative obstacles in the United States, Catalonia—after lengthy discussions—has become the first Spanish region to launch a pilot project for this method.

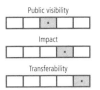

The two countries take different approaches to the electronic prescribing of pharmaceutical products. In the United States, the idea is to send an electronic prescription directly to the patient's pharmacist of choice. In Spain, doctors will in the future upload the prescription in a standard format for storage on a central database, where it will be accessible by any pharmacist. Both prescription systems are linked to the patient's electronic file so that doctors are provided with an overview of the medicines already prescribed.

Both countries want to achieve a significant improvement in the quality of the prescription of drugs. The health ministries see scope for improvement in the reduction of unwanted side effects of medicines or combinations of medicines, including allergic reactions and incorrect dosages. An American study from 1999 (Bates et al.) showed that prescription errors could be reduced by 86 percent with e-prescribing. This includes errors made by pharmacists who hand over the wrong drug because they cannot read the handwriting on the conventional prescription. The study also showed that the proportion of prescriptions issued in accordance with guidelines improved by 74 percentage points, from 14 percent to 88 percent.

Fewer mistakes when writing out prescriptions and fewer problems with side effects and incompatibility between drugs can contribute to a reduction in the overall costs for prescription medicines. Improved transparency also means that doctors take more care with their prescribing behavior. In Spain, chronic patients usually have to visit their general practitioner every time they need a repeat prescription. The new system stores the data and physicians can hand out repeat prescriptions to the chronically ill without another visit. The removal of this bureaucratic hurdle can lead to long-term cost reductions for the health system.

While industrial companies in the United States spend an average of USD 8,000 (5,957 euros) on information technology for each employee, the equivalent cost item for health institutions is only $1,000 (745 euros). Inappropriate legal incentives in the health sector have meant that technologies that could contribute to the safety of patients have not been introduced. The introduction of an electronic system for the prescription of drugs together with electronic health records is made more difficult by national security legislation. This prohibits doctors from accepting any sort of reward. Private sponsors are therefore prevented from making software, hardware, or training in the use of systems available to hospitals or physicians' offices without charge. The 2003 law on the modernization of the prescription of pharmaceutical products calls for the removal of legislation that prevents the influence of third-party support regarding the IT-infrastructure of health institutions. The Office of the Inspector General of the Department of Health issued regulations in early 2006 aimed at allowing the introduction of electronic patient files and e-prescribing by making it possible to accept nonmonetary goods and services. To solve problems in the IT infrastructure, a bill passed by the Senate aims at supporting the implementation of sophisticated health IT structures with about $160 million (119 million euros) in funds.

Because of the autonomy of its 17 individual regions with respect to health care, Spain faces particular challenges regarding the nationwide introduction of electronic prescription systems. Already in 2002, the Spanish Ministry of Science and Technology launched the PISTA project (Promotion and Identification of Emergent Services in Advanced Telecommunications). Each autonomous region must conclude a bilateral treaty with the Spanish Ministry of Health in order to receive funds for the implementation of an IT system. As the first region, Catalonia began a pilot project in January 2006 to introduce the electronic prescription of medicines. The test phase was concluded in June 2006, and the system is now available for users in the pilot area. A first evaluation was planned for the end of 2006. The electronic prescription system will then be introduced throughout Catalonia.

Catalonia: first region with e-prescribing

The greatest problem for both the United States and Spain is the secure transfer of data in a network system. In Spain, all the institutions involved have access to patients' personal data, which may infringe on the private sphere of the patients and could be subject to manipulation. However, experts in both countries expect to see an improvement in the security of the system in the coming years. They view the further development of technological systems in health care as a key element for the future.

Ensuring security

Sources and further reading:
Spain:
Sánchez, Elvira. "Electronic prescription pilot project in Catalonia." *Health Policy Monitor*, April 2006. www.hpm. org/survey/es/a7/4.

Generalitat de Catalunya. Departament de Salut. La Receta Electrónica en Cataluña (Rec@t), June 2006. www.gen cat.net/salut/depsan/units/sanitat/pdf/eseh2.pdf.

Generalitat de Catalunya. Departament de Salut. Catalunya conté l'increment de la despesa farmacèutica per segon any consecutiu. www.gencat.net/salut/depsan/units/sanitat/pdf/np160506.pdf.

United States:
Speaker, Elizabeth L. "Adoption of E-prescribing Technology." *Health Policy Monitor*, April 2006. www.hpm.org/survey/us/b7/4.

Bates, Davis W., Jonathan M. Teich, Joshua Lee, Diane Seger, Gilad J. Kuperman, Nell Ma'Luf, Deborah Boyle and Lucian Leape. "The Impact of Computerized Order Entry Systems on Medication Error Prevention." *Journal of the American Medical Informatics Association* 6(4): 313–321, 1999.

Bell, Douglas S., and Maria A. Friedman. "E-Prescribing and the Medicare Modernization Act of 2003." *Health Affairs*. 24(5): 1168, 2005.

Hartsfield, Shannon. "MMA and ePrescribing. New Compliance Standards for eHealth." *Food and Drug Law*. 2(1): 3–4, 2005.

United States Department of Health and Human Services. Office of the National Coordinator for Health Information Technology (ONC). www.hhs.gov/healthit/e-prescribing.html.

New Zealand:
Continued unlimited advertisement of medicines?

In New Zealand, direct-to-consumer marketing of medicines is under scrutiny. A consultation document was released by the Ministry of Health in March 2006 outlining three options for modification of the existing legislation and calling on interested parties to submit comments, and, if appropriate, make their own proposals.

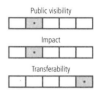

New Zealand and the United States are the only industrialized countries to allow direct-to-consumer advertising (DTCA) of prescription medicines. While most countries have legal restrictions on such advertising for drugs or ban it completely, New Zealand draws on its Bill of Rights, which protects freedom of speech, including the freedom to advertise.

The first option proposed by the health ministry would allow DTCA to continue, but with more stringent regulation. Self-regulation by the pharmaceutical companies would be subjected to closer inspection, with high penalties for breaches of the regulations.

The second option would continue to allow DTCA but with stricter requirements than envisaged under the joint Therapeutic Products Advertising Code. A third option would be to ban such advertising and also to regulate so-called disease-state advertising, which does not recommend any specific product.

In 2001, an opinion poll found that 40 percent of those questioned were in agreement with direct advertising for prescription medicines, with 34 percent in favor of a ban. On the basis of the poll's findings, the health ministry called for stricter provisions, but there was no change in the legislation. In 2003, a group of general practitioners presented the health ministry with a report in which they demanded a ban on drug advertising. The reason they advanced was the huge rise in advertising campaigns for

Direct-to-consumer advertising permitted under Bill of Rights

Three proposals for change

Previous evaluations without results

drugs and in particular for lifestyle products (see report in *Health Policy Developments*, issue 2).

The current initiative of the health ministry is based on neither the opinion poll nor the doctors' recommendations, but on the plans to create an Australia—New Zealand Therapeutic Products Authority in 2007. It would be possible for both countries to retain their existing policies toward advertising of prescription medicines, but the change opens up the possibility of reviewing current legislation and to make amendments.

Sources and further reading:
CHSRP. "Advertising of pharmaceuticals (2)." *Health Policy Monitor*, April 2006. www.hpm.org/survey/nz/a7/5.

Hoek Janet, Philip Gendall and John Calfee. "Direct-to-Consumer Advertising of Prescription Medicines in the United States and New Zealand: An analysis of regulatory approaches and consumer responses." *International Journal of Advertising* 23(2): 197–227, 2004.
Government of New Zealand, Ministry of Health. *Direct-to-Consumer Advertising of Prescription Medicines in New Zealand. Consultation Document*, March 2006. www.moh. govt.nz/moh.nsf/238fd5fb4fd 051844c 25666 9006aed57/ 8daa2bc24bcff5d9cc25712400778549?opendocument. www.moh.govt.nz/moh.nsf/pagesmh/5147?Open.

Disease prevention

Prevention is still playing a secondary role in health systems. In Germany, for example, only 0.5 percent of the gross domestic product was spent on prevention and public health in 2003. One problem is that the effects of prevention programs are usually assessed only over a long time scale. Another point is that prevention is directed at improving the health of the population in general but often requires the cooperation of individuals. An overview of methods and measures for prevention are presented here in brief. Selected current prevention strategies of individual countries are considered that may serve as a model for other countries.

Prevention measures can take a variety of forms and are generally divided into three groups: health promotion, health protection and disease prevention. Individually and combined, they have a positive influence on the health of the population and are targeted at specific illnesses (e.g., infectious diseases), risk factors (e.g., obesity), target groups (e.g., young people) and settings (e.g., schools).

Methods of prevention

Health promotion aims at encouraging people to adopt and maintain a healthful lifestyle. South Korea has established a prevention program that targets the lifestyles of the rural population and the elderly. The special feature of the approach is that Oriental medicine, diet and exercise, which the target group understands and accepts, are used in combination with Western, evidence-based preventative methods (see page 197). It is also important for the prevention debate in Europe that health promotion should take into account the needs and principles of the public if it is to be successful in the long term.

Health promotion, ...

Health protection involves preventive measures aimed at limiting the environmental factors that threaten health. Laws, regula-

... health protection, ...

193

Fig. 5: Prevention and the stages of disease

Course of disease	A	B	C	D
	Primary prevention	Secondary prevention	Tertiary prevention	

A–B	Period of increased risk
B	First observable pathophysiological changes
C	First changes perceivable by patient
D	Course can no longer be influenced

Primary prevention is directed at the prevention of illness by removing the causes. The target group for primary prevention is healthy with respect to the target disease.

Secondary prevention aims at identifying the disease at an early stage so that it can be treated. This makes possible an early cure (or at least the prevention of further deterioration). The target group for secondary prevention consists of people who are already ill without being aware of it, or who have an increased risk, or who have a genetic disposition.

Tertiary prevention is directed toward people who are already known to suffer from an illness. This is therefore a form of care. Tertiary prevention includes activities intended to cure, to ameliorate or to compensate. For example, the avoidance of complications or the prevention of progress of disease would be classed as tertiary prevention.

Source: Mackenbach and van der Maas 1999

tions and direct intervention in the environment can protect people against the negative influences of the environment. In addition to physical factors such as air, water and soil pollution, health protection also includes social components, such as the housing situation, the level of education and the social network (see issue 5, "Health and lifestyle").

... and disease prevention

The aim of disease prevention programs is to prevent avoidable disease or to identify diseases early (see figure 5). Possible measures include vaccination programs and screening. Australia has implemented a national screening program for the early recognition of bowel cancer. The target group for this measure is all Australians older than 55 (see page 198).

A trend toward holistic approaches

Effective strategies for the long-term improvement of public health often include various methods of prevention. Two prevention programs in New Zealand illustrate such multilevel approaches. A nationwide diabetes prevention program combines primary, secondary and tertiary interventions and thus reaches the entire target population (see page 200). A 10-year suicide prevention plan also operates at all three levels to reduce the country's very high suicide rates (see page 202). European countries should also consider extending preventive programs to include holistic approaches, because prevention is only really effective when measures reach the entire target group.

In many industrialized countries, a central problem with the implementation of holistic prevention programs at the national level is conflicting responsibilities. In Germany, for example, health promotion measures are governed by a nonmedical public institution (the Federal Center for Health Education), whereas the public health offices are responsible for health protection. Disease prevention is a medical matter, organized in various ways depending on the specialists involved. Breast cancer screening by mammography, for example, is not linked with the Breast Cancer Disease Management Program, which is aimed at tertiary prevention, resulting in overlapping efforts and redundancy.

Legal clarification of responsibilities

Switzerland has introduced legislation to make prevention a national topic. There too, prevention has been insufficiently promoted at the level of the cantons because of a lack of transparency and the unclear allocation of responsibilities (see page 205).

Despite the efforts to promote prevention, it often requires special situations before action is taken. In Israel, the stroke suffered by former Prime Minister Ariel Sharon drew attention to the topic of stroke prevention. Before this there had been little public interest, and patient organizations and neurologists had campaigned in vain for better prevention. Now various measures are to be adopted in a prevention program with three levels from healthy to ill in order to reduce the incidence of strokes and the severity of their effects (see page 207).

More prevention even without public pressure

Evaluations show differing results for prevention measures. Vaccinations for children are very effective and lead to considerable cost savings in the health system. The pilot study for bowel cancer screening in Australia has also been shown to be very cost-effective (see page 198). However, the cost-effectiveness of preventive measures suffers in comparison with therapeutic measures when examined using the discounting method favored among health economists, because expenses occur immediately and possible benefits at a much later date. Other prevention measures such as flu shots for healthy employees seem to have no effects, and some screening programs may even be counter-

Benefits of prevention

productive because of false-positive or false-negative results that may cause unnecessary stress and concern or lead to a false sense of security. A further factor influencing the effectiveness of prevention programs is the way they are conducted. A program that is effective under study conditions will be useless if it does not actually reach the public. There are therefore no clear answers regarding the benefits and the cost-effectiveness of prevention programs in general, and the results depend not only on the program but also on the way it is conducted. Current prevention programs can serve as a reference, but they must be adapted to the actual situation of the program in each case.

Sources and further reading:
Cyr, Nellie. *Health promotion, disease prevention and exercise epidemiology.* Dallas: University Press of America 2003.
German Federal Ministry of Health. Health Prevention. http://www.bmg.bund.de/cln_040/nn_617014/EN/Pre vention/prevention-node,param=.html_nnn=true.
Olsen, Jørn. Disease prevention and control of non-communicable diseases. In *Oxford Textbook of Public Health.* Fourth Edition, edited by Roger Detels, James McEwen, Robert Beaglhole and Heizo Tanaka. Oxford and New York: Oxford University Press 2002: 1811–1822.
Maas, Paul van der, and Johan Mackenbach (eds). *Volksgezondheid en gezondheidszorg.* Maarssen: Elsevier/Bunge 1999.
Rose, Geoffrey. *The strategy of preventive medicine.* Oxford, New York and Tokyo: Oxford University Press 1992.
World Health Organization Regional Office for Europe. *Gaining Health. The European strategy for the prevention and control of noncommunicable diseases.* Copenhagen, 2006. http://www.euro.who.int/document/E89306.pdf.

South Korea: Health promotion with traditional medicine

With its program for the promotion of health through Oriental medicine, the South Korean Ministry of Health and Welfare intends to improve the lifestyle of its population. In the future, public health centers will offer secondary prevention measures for certain risk groups.

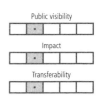

The program is aimed primarily at the rural population and the elderly. These groups tend to place their trust in traditional medicine, nutrition and movement, and are somewhat skeptical of Western methods. For this reason, doctors and nursing personnel are trying to develop community programs targeted toward the problems of each catchment area.

Secondary prevention for rural populations and the elderly

Overall, the idea of a more healthful lifestyle and thus better health is growing in importance in South Korea. Because the belief in traditional medicine is firmly anchored in the population, the Ministry of Health and Welfare has decided to link Western evidence-based programs with methods from traditional medicine. In this way the ministry hopes to increase acceptance.

Health promotion increasingly important

In the initial phase, 30 health centers are introducing health promotion programs. The ministry is planning to extend this to all centers in the country.

Thirty health centers introduce program

The government intends to fund the health promotion program with extra income from tobacco taxation. After a tax rise in 2005, the price for cigarettes almost doubled, and the share of tax rose from 8 eurocents to 1.63 euros per pack (see report in *Health Policy Developments,* issue 3).

Tobacco tax for prevention

The South Korean Medical Council, in which doctors oriented toward Western medicine predominate, views traditional health promotion with skepticism. But the Korean Association of Oriental Medicine supports it. With traditional practitioners now also able to work in the health centers, the Korean Association of Oriental Medicine sees good prospects for the development of ap-

Traditional doctors in health centers

proaches to health promotion that draw on traditional medicine, nutrition and movement. For its part, the Medical Council fears a loss of popularity of Western medicine and growing competition between the two approaches. With the projects still in the development stage, it is not yet clear what the effects of the combination of prevention and traditional medicine will be. The Medical Council, therefore, has not yet initiated any campaign against the health promotion program.

Sources and further reading:
Kwon, Soonman. "Health Promotion based on Traditional Medicine." *Health Policy Monitor,* April 2006. www.hpm. org/survey/kr/a7/2.

Ministry of Health and Welfare. Ministry opens Oriental medicine R&D centre, 2005. http://english.mohw.go.kr/ user.tdf?a=user.board.BoardApp&c=2002&seq=288& board_id=e_c1_news&mc=E_02_01&ctx=.

Australia: Bowel cancer screening for persons over 55

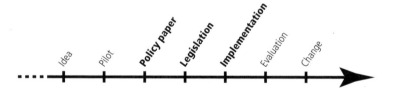

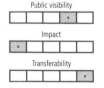

Since mid-2006, the Australian government has been introducing an initiative for national bowel cancer screening. By 2008, all Australians between the ages of 55 and 65 will be screened every two years. Bowel cancer is one of the most common types of cancer in Australia. The aim of the screening initiative is to reach the entire population at risk.

In the past, the capacity for colonoscopies in the public health service was limited, and the cost of a private inspection was high, particularly for the 55 percent of the population who do not have additional private insurance. The national government, which had already included bowel cancer prevention in its political program for the elections in 2004 as an important health policy target, made AUD $43.4 million (about 25.3 million euros) available for the implementation of the program until 2008.

Prevention in the past only for people with private health insurance

The prevention program consists of two stages. First, the target population is requested to take a stool sample at home and send this in for laboratory analysis. If the result of this fecal occult blood test is positive, then as a second step the general practitioner gets in touch with the patient and carries out more tests, including a colonoscopy.

A pilot project carried out in three locations in Australia has shown that 8 percent of all samples submitted were positive. Of those with a positive result, 55 percent underwent a colonoscopy, and 19 percent of these were found to have cancer in an early or advanced stage. According to the final report on the pilot project, 45.4 percent of the target population took part in the tests, but Aborigines and Torres Strait Islanders were underrepresented. The report called for a specific information campaign for these population groups.

Good response in pilot project

The pilot study showed that bowel cancer screening is cost-effective. For the target population between 55 and 74, the estimated costs for each extra year of life gained was AUD $24,000 (about 14,000 euros). The incremental cost-effectiveness for the pilot group (screening vs. no screening) was $20,000 (about 11,500 euros).

Screening is cost-effective

Until 2008, the national program will be subject to scientific supervision. In the event of a positive evaluation, it will be extended to all people over 55, and in the case of Aborigines all those over 45. The decision to extend the screening will be based only on clinical results and not on economic ones.

Extension depends on clinical results

The Australian Cancer Council supports the plans of the government, which it is advising on the topics of prevention, identification and treatment. On the basis of the pilot program, other experts also expect that screening will have a large effect on the early recognition of bowel cancer, making the program accessible to all the population and increasing the quality of care through treatment at an early stage.

Cancer Council and experts support the program

Sources and further reading:
van Gool, Kees. "Bowel Cancer Screening Program." *Health Policy Monitor*, April 2006. www.hpm.org/survey/au/a7/2.

Australian Government, Department of Health and Ageing. Australia's Bowel Cancer Screening Pilot and Beyond. Final Evaluation Report, October 2005. www.can cerscreening.gov.au/bowel/pdfs/eval_oct05.pdf.
Australian Government, Department of Health and Ageing. National Bowel Cancer Screening Program. www. cancerscreening.gov.au/bowel/bcaust/program.htm.
Liberal Party of Australia. The Howard Government Election 2004 Policy. Strengthening Cancer Care. www. liberal.org.au/2004_policy/acf3c25.pdf.

New Zealand: Let's Beat Diabetes

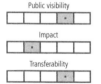

Public visibility

Impact

Transferability

Under the slogan "Let's Beat Diabetes," the health authority of Manukau County has developed an integral plan to structurally tackle the occurrence, consequences and costs of type 2 diabetes.

Demographic developments and an increase in obesity have made type 2 diabetes increasingly common in New Zealand. According to estimates, the numbers of type 2 diabetes patients will double in the next 20 years. The incidence is particularly high among Maoris. Whereas 8.5 percent of all non-Maoris over 45 have diabetes, the figure is 21 percent for Maoris. The socially disadvantaged also have a higher risk of developing type 2 diabetes. The reduction in the incidence of diabetes is one of the 13 health goals formulated by the health ministry in 1999.

The strategy of the Manukau health authority is holistic and involves three prevention approaches. Through primary, secondary and tertiary prevention, the incidence of type 2 diabetes is to be reduced effectively. To this end, an intersectoral plan has been developed that targets the various age groups individually. In addition to the national specifications, the plan also draws on international standards (best practices).

Primary, secondary and tertiary prevention

The plan consists of 10 fields of action. Goals and measures have been developed for each:

Ten fields of action

- Supporting community leadership and action
- Promoting behavioral change through social marketing
- Changing urban design to support healthful, active lifestyles
- Supporting a healthful environment through a food industry accord
- Strengthening health promotion coordination and activity
- Enhancing child services to reduce childhood obesity
- Developing an accord with schools to ensure that children are "fit, healthy and ready to learn"
- Supporting primary care-based prevention and early intervention
- Enabling vulnerable families to make healthful choices
- Improving service integration and care for advanced disease

The fields of action are being tackled together with partners from various sectors, including local governments, the food industry and representatives of cultural groups, schools, sports clubs, and public and private health institutions.

The program has an initial five year time-frame for implementation and NZD 10 million (about 4.8 million euros) has been allocated for this purpose. The program is supported by all the participants, including the food industry. The first evaluation of the program implementation was carried out in mid-2006. The participants agreed that full implementation of the prevention measures can lead to a sustainable reduction in the number of diabetes patients and thus improve the quality and the efficiency of health care.

Five-year plan

Sources and further reading:
CHSRP et al. "An inter-sectoral approach to diabetes." *Health Policy Monitor*, April 2006. www.hpm.org/survey/nz/a7/3.

Centers for Disease Control and Prevention. Framework for program evaluation in public health. *Mortality and Morbidity Weekly Report* 48(RR11): 1–40, 1999.

Manukau District Health Board. Let's Beat Diabetes: A Five Year Plan to Prevent and Manage Type 2 Diabetes in Counties. Manukau, 2005. www.letsbeatdiabetes.org. nz/file/LBD%205%20Year%20Strategic%20Overview. pdf.

Manukau District Health Board. Let's Beat Diabetes. Operational Plan 2005/2006, 2005. www.letsbeatdiabetes.org. nz/file/LBD%20Operational%20Plan%2005-06.pdf.

Government of New Zealand, Ministry of Health. Diabetes 2000. www.moh.govt.nz/moh.nsf/0/4735077ed3fd9b56cc 256a41000975ca/.

New Zealand: Suicide prevention strategy 2006–2016

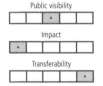

Public visibility

Impact

Transferability

In June 2006, the New Zealand government announced a suicide prevention plan. The aim of the government is to promote community initiatives to reduce both the incidence and social consequences of suicides.

In the coming 10 years, two five-year plans will be implemented, aimed at all age groups of the population. The project's primary focus is to develop strategies for institutions that could achieve much through prevention work. Among such institutions are schools, prisons, communities, the government and the media.

The first plan was to be published in December 2006. Among other things, the measures include early identification of suicide risks, support for the dependents of suicide victims, the extension of evidence-based research in the field, and support for people in crises.

In New Zealand, as in other countries, more people die by suicide than in road accidents. Of all OECD member states, New Zealand has the fourth-highest suicide rate for young people. Boys are almost three times more at risk than girls. Among adults, in contrast, the number of suicide attempts among women is double that among men. The main factors associated with suicide are socioeconomic status, cultural background, gender, age and place of residence. The goal is to cut the suicide rate in New Zealand by reducing inequalities. Prevention can also reduce stays in psychiatric clinics for people at risk of possible suicide, stays that otherwise cause considerable expense in the health system.

More suicides than traffic deaths

Because suicide is often the outcome of an accumulation of risk factors, tackling it is complex, and according to the health ministry it requires cooperation between sectors. Public and private organizations must be equally involved.

Suicide prevention requires a holistic approach

The cross-sectoral suicide prevention group, which is under the aegis of the health ministry, has a leading role to play, because it has already gained experience since 1999 in the implementation of measures for suicide prevention among young people.

Since it came to power, the Labour government has supported intersectoral strategies to fight diseases, and it is continuing to implement the national social agenda with this prevention program. Whereas public health experts support this approach, psychologists assert that it does not specifically target the early recognition of depression or provide for its pharmacological treatment. In order to overcome differences and to raise the quality of the program, the government has set up an external advisory group. It will observe and evaluate the work of the intersectoral suicide prevention group.

Suicide prevention as a social task

Sources and further reading:
CHSRP, Lisa Walton and Janet Fanslow. "Suicide Prevention Strategy." *Health Policy Monitor*, April 2006. www.hpm.org/survey/nz/a7/4.

Government of New Zealand, Ministry of Health. New Zealand Suicide Prevention Strategy 2006–2016. Wellington, 2006. www.moh.govt.nz/moh.nsf/pagesmh/4904/$File/suicide-prevention-strategy-2006-2016.pdf.

Government of New Zealand, Ministry of Health. New Zealand Youth Suicide Prevention Strategy. Wellington, 1998. www.moh.govt.nz/moh.nsf/49b6bf07a4b7346dcc256fb300005a51/c3dc5fc2d9a05cf1cc2570a50082edb4?opendocument.

Government of New Zealand, Ministry of Health. Suicide Prevention in New Zealand. A contemporary perspective. Social explanations for suicide in New Zealand. Wellington, 2005. www.moh.govt.nz/moh.nsf/0/E426CB2D56854BCC256FFF00170256/$File/suicideprevention-socialexplanations.pdf.

Government of New Zealand, Ministry of Health. The New Zealand Health Strategy. Wellington, 2000. www.moh.govt.nz/moh.nsf/49b6bf07a4b7346dcc256fb300005a51/fb62475d5d911e88cc256d42007bd67e?opendocument.

Switzerland: Law on prevention
to provide transparency and equality

In September 2005, the Swiss Department of Internal Affairs (EDI) started a project to strenghten the role of prevention and health promotion at the national level alongside the three established pillars of treatment, care and rehabilitation. The background for this initiative is an increased awareness about prevention in the population and in the media. Previously, national health-policy decisions had concentrated exclusively on curative treatment and its funding. Preventive measures are the responsibility of the cantons, and the result is that the provisions differ considerably among them.

In March 2005, a national commission of experts was given the task of establishing the framework for national prevention measures. The commission, under the name Prevention and Health Promotion: PPS2010 should first discuss the possibilities for prevention at a national level and form strategic alliances. Prevention should adopt a cross-sectoral approach and be implemented throughout the country. Transparency of both the activities and the funding, therefore, played a central role, and the commission also developed a strategy to monitor the results and compare them with the goals that had been formulated.

Experts' commission for Prevention and Health Promotion …

In March 2006, the commission published a strategy paper describing the overall objectives of and the possibilities for an approach to introduce legislation. The commission wanted a law that would firmly anchor prevention at the national level. A central point is the cross-sectoral approach, which combines primary and secondary prevention measures. The planned law is intended to ensure transparency while clearly defining duties and funding responsibilities.

… develops a prevention law

Public institutions (local authorities, cantons, the national government) and the private sector (service providers, NGOs, businesses) would be integrated in the new prevention strategy. Each partner would be involved financially in the health-promotion programs, which are aimed at the entire population.

Over the past 30 years, repeated initiatives in Switzerland have called for a legal basis for prevention. They were dropped because of lacking consent among the political actors involved. The federal system, in which the cantons assume separate responsibility, and the principle of subsidiarity, by which private or social institutions assume responsibility for public tasks, also contribute to a lack of coordination.

The creation of a national commission and the move to pass a national prevention law are the first steps toward uniform regulation of prevention and health promotion throughout the country. In order to avoid opposition leading to the rejection of the law, the commission presented a number of regulatory solutions to 140 public and private actors, who then had the opportunity to suggest improvements. In June 2006, the commission's final report was presented to the Department of Internal Affairs for consideration. The department was supposed to decide on further steps by the ende of 2006. At the time of reporting, this decision is still pending.

Only if the legal framework is provided and the public and private actors are given clear remits will effective nationwide prevention be possible. It will be necessary to establish the transparent, reliable regulation of finances, because prevention work usually involves long-term programs. If these preconditions are met, it will be possible to achieve considerable improvements in the public health sector, because in addition to the effects of national prevention campaigns, more social equality will be achieved. The reduction in the overlap of responsibilities can lead to the long-term simplification and improvement of the health system. But until specific prevention plans have been presented, the experts in Switzerland are not clear whether a prevention law will also lead to savings, although it seems certain that cutting back inefficiencies in the allocation of responsibilities and the distribution of funds can reduce costs.

Sources and further reading:
Bolgiani, Iva. "National experts' commission for Health Promotion." *Health Policy Monitor*, April 2006. www. hpm.org/survey/ch/a7/3.

The Federal Assembly, The Swiss Parliament. Prévention et promotion de la santé. Renforcer la transparence et la coordination, 2005. http://search.parlament.ch/e/home page/cv-geschaefte.htm?gesch_id=20053161.
Federal Office of Public Health FOPH. Projet Nouvelle réglementation de la prévention et de la promotion de la santé en Suisse. www.bag.admin.ch/themen/gesund heitspolitik/00388/01811/01820/index.html?lang=fr.
Health Promotion Switzerland: Long term strategy, January, 2006. www.promotionsante.ch/common/files/strat egy/N182087_LangfristigeStrategie_en.pdf.

Israel: Sharon's illness raises interest in stroke prevention

The stroke suffered by Prime Minister Sharon in January 2006 led to a marked increase in public awareness about this disease. The media coverage has prompted the Israeli health ministry to appoint a group of experts to formulate proposals for improving the care of stroke patients. The objective is the promotion of stroke prevention and the improvement of the quality of care for stroke victims. The group of experts developed regulations to better reach the risk group (in the sense of primary and secondary prevention), to raise public awareness about the first signs of a stroke, and to ensure rapid assistance in the event of an apoplec-

tic insult. Strokes are the third most common cause of death, and
two-thirds of those affected are over 65.

Best prevention:
healthful lifestyle Primary prevention measures against apoplexy relate to a healthful lifestyle (avoidance of smoking, weight control and physical
activity). Risk groups, such as people with hypertension and ven-
tricular fibrillation, should be treated in accordance with standardized guidelines so as to reduce their risk of a stroke (secondary
prevention). When stroke patients are presented, hospital doctors
should use specific guidelines for their treatment, and measures
should be in place to prevent a recurrence (tertiary prevention).
These measures include the provision of special stroke units, and
treatment with a tissue plasminogen activator (TPA). Studies
have shown that the administration of TPA within the first three
hours of a stroke can effectively prevent long-term damage. In
Israel, TPA is hardly used at all.

Sharon stimulates
media interest The driving forces behind the initiatives are neurologists and
patient representatives who saw Sharon's stroke as an opportunity to launch a media debate about the lack of public awareness
and common definitions for care. In contrast to cancer or heart
disease, investment in the prevention of strokes has been low.
The National Stroke Association had already presented the health
ministry with guideline proposals in 2003, but the ministry did
not approve these for further dissemination. After Sharon's stroke
and the media interest it generated, the ministry has now issued
guidelines for prevention and treatment measures to health insurers, hospitals, emergency services, other health-service providers,
and the public.

Rapid
implementation
of prevention
measures All those involved—health ministry, hospitals, patient associations, neurologists—plead for more prevention. However, the
health insurance funds raise the point that they have inadequate
resources for prevention services. They also believe that stroke
treatment is already of a high standard.

Experts expect that successful public awareness campaigns
and further training can lead to a substantial improvement in
stroke treatment. Guidelines lead to a reduction in the difference
in treatment. In the long term, prevention measures should also
lead to savings. The costs of modern methods of treatment are
higher in the short term, but they can make lengthy after-treat-
ment unnecessary. It remains to be seen how the wider distribu-

tion of such guidelines in the wake of the stroke suffered by Prime Minister Sharon will actually improve prevention measures. Nor is it yet clear how preventive measures will be implemented alongside treatment standards.

Sources and further reading:
Bentur, Netta, and Revital Gross. "Regulations for improving care of stroke patients." *Health Policy Monitor*, April 2006. www.hpm.org/survey/is/a7/2.

Progress in protecting nonsmokers

Fewer and fewer adults are reaching for a cigarette on a daily basis. There has been a marked decline in the number of adult smokers in most OECD countries over the past 20 years. The downward trend has been reinforced by a bundle of interacting measures that include information campaigns, bans on tobacco advertising, and increased taxes and import duties. The proportion of people smoking in Germany, for example, has gone down from about 35 percent in 1980 to 24.3 percent in 2003 and now lies slightly below the OECD average of 25.5 percent. This is a remarkable success in the reduction of tobacco consumption, but it is still not much in comparison, for example, with Sweden, Canada and the United States, countries where only 15 percent to 17 percent of the adult population still smoke (www.oecd.org/dataoccd/55/6/37006838.pdf).

For some time, tobacco consumption and its negative health consequences have been fought by a variety of regulatory measures. As a rule, these include

How tobacco consumption can be reduced

- Pricing policies: taxes, minimum duties, minimum prices
- Communication: limitations on advertising, product displays and marketing (for example a ban on the use of adjectives such as "mild" or "light"). Also requirements for obligatory labeling on the packaging, for example health warnings and details of the names and amounts of the substances contained
- Packaging: minimum size of packs of cigarettes
- Distribution: age limits on the purchase of cigarettes, fitting out cigarette vending machines with appropriate youth protection technology
- Consumption: smoking bans in various places

The effectiveness of measures to reduce tobacco consumption
has been variously demonstrated (see table 3). At the same time,
packages of measures have proved more effective than individual
regulations. Anti-tobacco regulations should therefore be as comprehensive as possible and at the same time use a number of
instruments (price, distribution, communication, etc.).

Table 3: Effects of anti-smoking measures on prevalence of smokers

Measure	Effect on prevalence of smokers
Price increase by 10 percent	Decline of four percentage points in countries with high per capita income
Ban on smoking at work	Decline of five to 10 percentage points
Bans on smoking in pubs, restaurants and other public places	Decline of two to four percentage points
Advertising ban	Decline of six percentage points if ban is absolute
Health warning on cigarette packs	In the Netherlands, 28 percent of all 13- to 18-year-olds said they smoked less as a result of health warnings; in Belgium, eight percent of those asked said they smoked less because of warnings
Media campaigns	Percentage of smokers declines by five to 10 percentage points, depending on how the campaigns are targeted at certain groups
Withdrawal measures; subsidies for treatment	Decline of one to two percentage points after two years, depending on the spectrum of people registered

Source: European Network for Smoking Prevention. Effective tobacco control in
28 European countries, October 2004. www.ensp.org/files/effectivefinal2.pdf

Public opinions on
the effectiveness
of anti-smoker
measures To be effective, a campaign must reach the public. In a survey
commissioned by the European Union, 83 percent of Europeans
who were asked could recall an anti-smoking campaign. In Germany (82 percent) and Finland (84 percent), the proportion of
those who could recall such a campaign was somewhat higher
than in Austria (73 percent), although no details were provided
of the type of campaigns, their duration or their number in the
countries named (European Commission 2006).

212

All smokers and ex-smokers in the European Union countries estimated that the campaigns had little effect on their actual behavior; 68 percent of smokers and former smokers responding said they had not been persuaded by the campaigns to give up smoking.

In principle, the majority of people in Europe favor a ban on smoking in public buildings. But the degree of approval depends on the location in question. Thus 86 percent favored a ban on smoking in offices and workplaces in buildings, and 84 percent approved of a smoking ban in all other enclosed public rooms. However, a much lower proportion (56 percent of Europeans) favored smoking bans in pubs, bars and restaurants. Regarding only pubs and bars, only 40 percent of Europeans said they wanted a smoking ban.

But the situation looks different if the ban is restricted to smoking in restaurants. A large majority of those asked in most countries favors a ban. In Germany, about 70 percent approved; in the United Kingdom more than 80 percent. Austrians are the most reserved when it comes to a smoking ban in restaurants; still more than 60 percent approved.

Fig. 6: Approval of a smoking ban in restaurants in EU member states

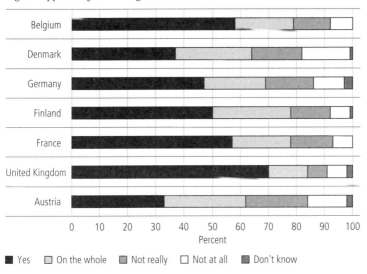

Source: European Commission 2006.

213

Fig. 7: Approval in the EU member states for a smoking ban in bars and pubs

Fig. 7: Approval in the EU member states for a smoking ban in bars and pubs

Country	0	10	20	30	40	50	60	70	80	90	100
Czech Republic											
Belgium											
Denmark											
Germany											
Finland											
France											
United Kingdom											
Portugal											
Austria											
Ireland											
Sweden											
Italy											

Percent

■ Yes □ On the whole ■ Not really □ Not at all ■ Don't know

Source: European Commission 2006.

In addition to the differences among the countries, agreement also depended on whether the interviewee smoked. While almost 88 percent of people who had never smoked and 83 percent of ex-smokers supported a smoking ban in restaurants, the approval among smokers was much lower, at only 55 percent, although this means that even in this group a majority supported the smoking ban. Among smokers of self-rolled cigarettes, the approval was only 48 percent.

... but disagreement about smoking in pubs and bars Public support for a ban on smoking in pubs and bars shows quite considerable variations among the European countries. In Italy (88 percent), Sweden (82 percent) and Ireland (82 percent), a large majority of the population supports the ban. In the Czech Republic (35 percent), Austria (42 percent), Finland (41 percent) and Germany (46 percent), the degree of support is much lower. It is interesting that rigid bans were introduced in the first group of countries some years ago—and that, after initial skepticism, more and more people have come to accept them.

A higher percentage of women (66 percent) support the ban on smoking in pubs and bars than men (57 percent). Like the smoking ban in restaurants, the ban on smoking in pubs and bars

214

has the support of the majority of nonsmokers but is only approved by 35 percent of smokers.

Sources and further reading:
European Network for Smoking Prevention. Effective tobacco control in 28 European countries, October 2004. www.ensp.org/files/effectivefinal2.pdf.

Health & Consumer Voice, Newsletter on foot safety, health and consumer policy from the European Commission's Health and Consumer Protection DG. Special Edition on Tobacco, May 2005. http://ec.europa.eu/dgs/health_consumer/consumervoice/cvsp_52005_en.pdf.

European Commission. Special Eurobarometer 239: Attitudes of Europeans towards tobacco. Fieldwork: September–December 2005. Publication: January 2006. http://ec.europa.eu/health/ph_information/documents/ebs_239_en.pdf.

OECD-Gesundheitsdaten 2006. Deutschland im Vergleich. www.oecd.org/dataoecd/55/6/37006838.pdf.

WHO Regional Office for Europe. Tobacco-free Europe. www.euro.who.int/eprise/main/who/progs/tob.

WHO Regional Office for Europe. Tobacco Control Database. data.euro.who.int/tabacco/?TabID=2402.

215

Finland: Smoking ban in bars and restaurants

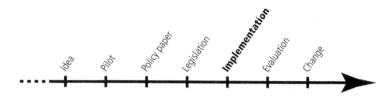

Public visibility

Impact

Transferability

Protection for staff and customers

Protests from bar and restaurant owners

In June 2006 Finland reformed its tobacco law, and as a result smoking has been banned in bars and restaurants since June 2007. An exception is made for enclosed, ventilated smoking rooms, although neither eating nor drinking is permitted in those places. Before the law was amended, smoking was permitted in designated open areas of pubs and restaurants.

With the reform, the lawmakers aim at protecting employees and nonsmoking customers from the negative effects of passive smoking on health. In Finland, smoking had already been banned at all workplaces except for restaurants and pubs.

Both the Ministry of Social Affairs and Health and the National Public Health Institute have supported the amendment to the law. Some employer organizations and trade unions have cooperated in formulating the proposal for greater protection against passive smoking in restaurants.

In particular, the owners of small bars have protested against the ban on smoking. They maintain that it would be impossible or too expensive to create a separate room for smokers. Because they have not taken any steps in the past for the protection of nonsmokers, they will have to implement the reform by June 2007. Larger pubs and restaurants which had already taken steps to provide separate smoking areas under the earlier legislation will be given until July 2009 to implement the more extensive measures. The lawmakers justify this two-year extension by saying that larger pubs and restaurants had already been required to invest in technical provisions to prevent the spread of smoke under the previous amendment to the tobacco legislation in 2000. Now, proprietors are worried that their guests will not spend as much time in pubs and restaurants as in the past.

In 2005, 60 percent of the Finnish population supported a ban on smoking in pubs and restaurants. The reform will have a considerable effect on both active and passive smoking in pubs, bars and restaurants. It is probable that a majority of pubs and restaurants will not be able to make arrangements for separate smoking rooms and therefore will be entirely smoke-free.

Majority of population for smoking ban

The passage of the legislation marked the conclusion of a long process. Until 2000, smoking had been allowed in pubs, bars and restaurants without restriction. Following an amendment to the law, it was then only allowed in specific areas. In total, the space designated for smokers was not allowed to account for more than half the total floor space of the pub or restaurant. In addition, the proprietor was required to introduce technical provisions (e.g., dividing walls, effective ventilation) to prevent the smoke from spreading to the nonsmoking area of the pub or restaurant. An exception was made if the total floor space was less than 50 square meters. In such cases, smoking was still allowed in the pub or restaurant, because it was considered impossible or impractical to introduce measures to stop the spread of smoke with so little space. However, because it is evident that neither separation into smoking and nonsmoking areas nor technical provisions suffice to protect staff and guests effectively against passive smoke, the law was amended again with the latest reform.

Long road to a smoking ban

The idea for smoking bans in pubs and restaurants and useful experience about the implementation came from Ireland and Norway. Preparations for bans on smoking had been under way in these countries for a long period, and they were implemented in 2004. The experience was largely positive. Italy and Sweden have already also introduced similar bans.

Ireland and Norway as models

Sources and further reading:
Vuorenkoski, Lauri. "Ban on smoking in pubs and restaurants." *Health Policy Monitor*, October 2006. www.hpm. org/survey/fi/a8/1.

Austria: Pricing policies, smoking bans and telephone quitline to reduce tobacco consumption

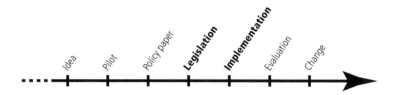

Public visibility

Impact

Transferability

Tobacco tax and minimum prices

Smoking ban with exceptions

"Quitline"

With increased tobacco taxes and minimum prices for tobacco products, the Austrian government in the past two years has created additional financial disincentives for smokers. In addition, fines were introduced for people who fail to respect bans on smoking or who do not designate no-smoking areas in pubs and restaurants. A free hotline has also been introduced for all Austria to support smokers who wish to give up smoking.

Taxes on tobacco products have been increased many times in Austria, most recently in 2005 by 18 eurocents per pack. In May 2006, a legal minimum retail price was set at 3.25 euros per pack, which purchasers have had to pay since August 2006. The number of young people who smoke has been growing in recent years, and the international literature shows that in particular the young are very sensitive to rising cigarette prices (ENSP 2004).

In connection with the Health Reform Act 2005 (see *Health Policy Developments,* issue 4, "Organizational reform"), a ban on smoking was introduced in all public buildings (although a series of exceptions was also made) and a ban on advertising for tobacco products (except poster and cinema advertising) was implemented. The latter has also been banned since January 1, 2007. In addition, the law requires the designation of places where smoking is banned. Since January 1, 2007, the failure to display signs showing nonsmoking zones can result in a fine of up to 720 euros.

In cooperation between the Association of Austrian Social Insurers and most of the federal states, a telephone hotline has been introduced that provides smokers who want to stop smoking with easy access to advice from certified psychologists. The "smoker telephone" can be called up at the cost of a local call from anywhere in Austria, even though the states of Salzburg and Tyrol are not taking part. The cooperation project is funded by income from tobacco taxation, the investment costs are borne by the sickness funds, and the operating costs are split between the social insurers and the states. With this initiative, Austria has become a member of the European Network of Quitlines, founded in 2001, which currently has 27 member countries. It is supported by the European Commission and cooperates with the European Network for Smoking Prevention. Its objectives are to promote the exchange of information and best practices about the telephone counseling of smokers (www.enqonline.org/public/aboutus.php).

Because cooperation among the various actors in the field of health promotion in Austria is rare, the agreement between most of the states and the social insurers about countrywide telephone counseling is a significant innovation. The success of the Quitline will also depend on the frequency and the extent to which the telephone counseling service is actually used. This means that evaluation will be required, and the scientific advisory board for the smoker telephone will be responsible for this.

The European Commission announced in April 2006 that it would be starting infringement procedures against Austria, Belgium, France, Italy and Ireland because of their minimum price regulations. The Commission asserts that minimum prices would distort competition and place an impermissible limitation on the right of the manufacturers to determine the prices of their products.

European Commission censures minimum prices

Although there is unity among the relevant stakeholders about the need for antismoking policies, opinions differ widely about the right strategies and measures to be adopted. In particular, the introduction of price thresholds in May 2006 was a much controverted matter.

The Austrian Social Democratic Party also regards the introduction of minimum prices as the wrong signal, and furthermore one which is in breach of EU legislation. It argues for a minimum consumer tax on tobacco products in combination with a lower limit on the profit margin for the manufacturer. Taxation exceeding this should be used for health prevention. In this context, it is often noted that revenues from the taxation on tobacco, which are intended to be used for prevention and public education, are proving to be very much lower than expected because of

Will black markets flourish because of minimum prices?

the increase in cigarette smuggling. Furthermore, the Social Democrats are also calling for an evaluation of government measures for the protection of nonsmokers in pubs, bars and restaurants.

Representatives of Austria Tobacco and British American Tobacco see the introduction of minimum prices as illegal intervention in free competition. Furthermore they—along with the Freedom Party of Austria—maintain that minimum prices are stimulating the black market.

Price thresholds necessary but not sufficient

The Green Alternative party, the Austrian Medical Council, the Association of Social Insurers and the tobacco retailers support the introduction of lower limits for the prices of tobacco products. They view price instruments as a more effective way of reducing the numbers of young smokers than the imposition of smoking bans. For these parties and actors, the measures implemented by the government do not go far enough. The Green party and the Medical Council find it necessary to provide more comprehensive protection for nonsmokers, in particular in the hotel and gastronomy sector, by a complete ban on smoking.

Are minimum prices socially unfair?

Price differences for cigarettes place a disproportionate burden on households with low incomes. Whereas minimum prices very probably discourage young people from starting to smoke, they could reinforce social inequalities. Currently, there are no studies in Austria about the influence of health promotion measures on the relevant behavior of specific socioeconomic groups.

Chamber of Commerce prefers voluntary undertakings in small pubs and restaurants

The Austrian Chamber of Commerce is against a binding ban on smoking in pubs, bars and restaurants. In a voluntary agreement with the Ministry of Health, the Chamber of Commerce has undertaken to ensure that no-smoking zones will be introduced in premises with less than 75 square meters of floor space. Forty percent of the capacity should be free from smoke. With this proposal, the Chamber of Commerce was responding to a call from the Medical Council that the prevalence of smoking should be reduced as a first step before a complete ban on smoking in bars and restaurants is imposed.

Sources and further reading:
Hofmarcher, Maria M. and Gerald Sirlinger. "Austria's anti-smoking strategies." *Health Policy Monitor*, October 2006. www.hpm.org/survey/at/a8/1.

Bundesministerium für Gesundheit und Frauen. *Rauchverhalten in Österreich – Ergebnisse unterschiedlicher Quellen.* Vienna, 2004 [available only in German].

Bundesministerium für Gesundheit und Frauen. Bundesgesetz über das Herstellen und das Inverkehrbringen von Tabakerzeugnissen sowie die Werbung für Tabakerzeugnisse und den Nichtraucherschutz (Tabakgesetz). Vienna, 2006. www.bmgf.gv.at/cms/site/attachments/3/0/7/CH0031/CMS1157719354616/14)_tabakgesetz_konsolidiert_i_d_g_f_.pdf (October 2006) [available only in German].

Dür, Wolfgang, Kristina Fürth, Katrin Indra and Monika Wimmer. Mädchen, Burschen, Rauchen. Gemeinsamkeiten der Geschlechter bei ihren RaucherInnenkarrieren. In *Männer, Frauen, Sucht.* Edited by Irmgard Eisenbach-Stangl, Susanne Lentner and Rudolf Mader. Vienna, 2004 [available only in German].

Euorpean Network of Quitlines. www.enqonline.org/public/aboutus.php.

Hofmarcher, Maria M., and Herta Rack. Austria. Health system review. *Health Systems in Transition* (8) 3 2006. 1–247.

ENSP – European Network for Smoking Prevention. Effective Tobacco Prevention Policies in 28 European Countries. 2004, www.ensp.org/files/effectivefinal2.pdf (October 2006)

Pelikan, Jürgen M., Christina Dietscher, Peter Nowak, Karl Krajic, Thomas Stidl and Hermann Schmied. *Projekt Österreichisches Netzwerk Gesundheitsfördernder Krankenhäuser. Endbericht 2004.* Vienna, 2004 [available only in German].

Newsflash

United States: California stem cell research program

In November 2004, Proposition 71 was approved in California—with the aim of providing USD 3 billion (about 2.2 billion euros) in funding for embryonic stem cell research in California through the sale of state funding bonds. The initiative empowered the state to establish a California Institute for Regenerative Medicine (CIRM) authorized to regulate stem cell research and to provide funding for the research facilities. The CIRM is monitored by an independent citizens' oversight committee (ICOC).

The stem cell research program has the goal of promoting the further development of stem cell research in California, making the state a leader in the field. The long-term goals would be to develop ways of treating chronic illnesses, create employment opportunities, and reduce expenditure on health care.

Under the Bush administration, a ban was put in place in 2001 on the use of federal funds for research on embryonic stem cell lines more recent than August 2001. But older stem cell lines are of only limited use for research and sometimes of no use at all. This means that effective research in this field is dependent on private funds or funds from the states. Embryonic stem cell research stagnated markedly in the following years. In 2004, California was the first state that sought legislation to promote the

California in the lead

Federal law against stem cell research

223

research within its borders. A series of other states, among them Michigan, Nebraska and Florida, are following the example of California.

Bush vetoes
relaxing ban on
stem cell research In May 2005, the U.S. House of Representatives approved a bill to remove the regulation of embryonic stem cell research. The Senate approved the bill in July 2006. President Bush vetoed the bill, and the attempt to override his veto failed.

Socially divisive However, the promotion of embryonic stem cell research is also potentially divisive in California. Its supporters include the California government, researchers, research institutions, bioethicists, the biotechnology industry and private donors. The government itself, however, though supporting the measure, says that state monitoring is inadequate. A bill to impose complete transparency about the allocation of research funds failed to gain enough support. The opponents include interest groups who are active for the rights of taxpayers and consumers and who support the rights of the unborn.

Numerous lawsuits
against research
program The opponents have filed various lawsuits in recent years—at first against the research promotion program, and after this had been accepted, against the legality of the newly established institutions and their authority to distribute funds without state control. The decisions so far have turned out in favor of the stem cell research program and its institutions. New lawsuits are pending, and in the opinion of experts these will continue to keep the courts busy in 2007.

Patent dispute
unresolved CIRM also is facing a legal battle initiated by the University of Wisconsin Alumni Research Foundation. This research association, established by former members of the University of Wisconsin, claims that three patents it holds give it the rights to the use of all embryonic stem cell lines in the United States. The foundation hopes to secure for itself a share of all revenues generated on the basis of discoveries made using its patented methods. Two public interest groups have submitted a petition to annul these patents, because earlier patents and other scientific publications already describe methods with which embryonic stem cells can be gained from various animals. The U.S. Patent Office has recently agreed to examine the situation.

CIRM caught
in limbo As long as the cases are before the courts, CIRM is not able to mobilize the USD 3 billion promised to it. Its room to maneuver

is therefore limited. Until CIRM is able to act freely without restrictions, supporters are providing bridging funds. These include the state of California itself, which through Governor Schwarzenegger has promised $150 million, and private donors. In addition, the CIRM financial committee has approved the sale of bonds with a value of $200 million to finance CIRM for the next two years. At the time of writing, private foundations had already bought bonds for $14 million.

CIRM has announced a 10-year strategy and a financial plan that has been informally approved by the state government. This plan envisages allocating research funds of startup aid for stem cell research and for setting up a statewide embryo bank.

Ten-year strategy and financing plan

In April 2006, CIRM awarded the first research funds totaling USD 12.1 million to 16 research institutions. The aim is to provide postdoctoral and postgraduate positions in stem cell research for 169 promising young scientists. A further 70 grants totaling $151 million will be provided to scientists who are already successful in stem cell research, researchers who are starting up in the field and need training, and special stem cell research laboratories. In October 2006, CIRM launched the first call for applications. In response it received 232 submissions for the 30 research grants with a combined value of $24 million.

First allocation of research funds

Stem cell research is an emerging field, and future applications are still unclear. It is not clear whether the hopes that many people are placing in this research will be realized, nor is it clear what (ethical) risks the research may involve. But it seems certain that the disputes between opponents and supporters will continue, and California will do all it can to establish and extend its position as a leading location for stem cell research.

No end to the conflicts in sight

Sources and further reading:
Schulz, Anke Therese, and Carol Medlin. "California Stem Cell Research Program (4)." *Health Policy Monitor*, March 2006. www.hpm.org/survey/us/c7/1.
Schulz, Anke Therese, and Carol Medlin. "California Stem Cell Research Program (3)." *Health Policy Monitor*, October 2005. www.hpm.org/survey/us/c6/5.

Weston, Sarah, and Carol Medlin. "California Stem Cell Research Program (2)." *Health Policy Monitor*, April 2005. www.hpm.org/survey/us/c5/5.
Kolb, Carol, and Carol Medlin. "California Stem Cell Research Program." *Health Policy Monitor*, April 2004. www.hpm.org/survey/us/c3/3.

Alliance for Stem Cell Research. www.curesforcalifornia.com/.
California Healthline. Stem Cell Research New Archives. www.californiahealthline.org/index.cfm?Action=dsp Archive&classCD=CL526&daysHist=8000.
California Institute for Regenerative Medicine. www.cirm.ca.gov/.
California Stem Cell Report Blog. californiastemcellreport.blogspot.com/.
Center for Genetics and Society. www.genetics-and-society.org/index.asp.

Canada: Will the government abandon healthcare guarantees?

Public visibility

Impact

Transferability

People worried about their health care

The newly elected conservative government of Canada has apparently decided to delete the much-discussed introduction of healthcare guarantees from its list of political priorities.

For years people have been expressing grave concerns about waiting lists in Canada's tax-funded healthcare system, which is managed by the provinces, although there have been no details available about which patients wait, how long they wait, and what effects the waiting times have on their health. The shortage of data also means that it is not possible to estimate whether long

226

waiting times are primarily due to shortages of personnel and equipment or to poor management of the waiting lists.

By means of care guarantees, patients should be given the right to receive treatment for certain specified illnesses within a given, evidence-based waiting time. If the patients do not receive care within this period, then they are entitled to have treatment outside the Canadian public system (e.g., privately or in the United States) at the cost of the provincial health system, or they can go to court to enforce the right. The intent has been to motivate the provincial governments and service providers to increase their capacities, to develop clinical standards with which the problem of waiting times can be measured more effectively, and to begin to solve the problem actively. Right to prompt care

In 2002, the topic of care guarantees was raised for the first time by Senator Kirby in the report "The Health of Canadians— the federal role." Kirby based his recommendations on the Swedish experience with care guarantees. In the same year the care guarantees were rejected in a report of the Commission on the Future of the Canadian Health System. Most of those involved are also skeptical about whether such an approach can be made to work in the highly decentralized Canadian health system. The Kirby Report had said nothing about how the care guarantees could be developed and implemented. Since then the care guarantees have been a never ending story—one in which interest has been dwindling. On the agenda since 2002

In the 2006 elections, the topic was included in the election platforms of both the Liberals and the Conservatives. After their election victory, the new Conservative government declared their intention to introduce wait-time guarantees, even though the previous Liberal government had provided additional funds for the reduction of waiting times for cancer treatments, coronary bypass surgery, hip and knee replacements, cataract operations, and certain radiological imaging, and there were increasing signs that these measures were having an effect. Care guarantees in the elections

For a long time it remained unclear how the government intended to implement healthcare guarantees and who would bear the financial risks. The provincial governments refused to accept the guarantees as long as the federal government in Ottawa gave no assurances about funding. The federal government, for its Unclear implementation

227

part, argued that the provinces and territories would have to use the additional funds paid out in earlier years to reduce waiting times as required under the proposed wait-time guarantees. The conflict led to an impasse, and Ottawa moved the guarantee lower down its list of political priorities.

Resort to private sector? Although the healthcare guarantees seem to be a popular idea, the political decision makers are not in a position to present a proposal that is acceptable to all parties. It is therefore unlikely that much progress will be made in this matter in the near future. It is possible that the Canadian people will increasingly lose trust in their health system and in the ability of the government to regulate it and will turn instead to alternatives in the privately financed provision of services.

Sources and further reading:
McIntosh, Tom. "Federal Government Abandons (?) Care Guarantees". *Health Policy Monitor,* October 2006. www.hpm.org/survey/ca/a8/1.

Fooks, Cathy, and Lisa Maslove. "A guarantee of timely care." *Health Policy Monitor,* October 2003. www.hpm.org/survey/ca/a2/2.

Fooks, Cathy, and Lisa Maslove. "Health Care Guarantee Proposal." *Health Policy Monitor,* April 2003. www.hpm.org/survey/ca/a1/5.

McIntosh, Tom, and Renee Torgerson. The Taming of the Queue III: Wait Measurement, Monitoring and Management—Where the Rubber Hits the Road. Ottawa: Canadian Policy Research Networks, 2006.

Senate of Canada. Standing Committee on Social Affairs, Science and Technology (Hon. Michael J. Kirby, Chair). The Health of Canadians—the Federal Role. Volume Five: Principles and Recommendations for Reform (parts 1 and 2). Ottawa: Parliament of Canada, 2002.

"Harper's New Game. Hide the Priority." *Maclean's* July 13, 2006. www.macleans.ca/columnists/article.jsp?content=20060724_130433_130433.

Slovenia: Public debate about the privatization of primary care

Although there are currently heated debates about the privatization process in the Slovenian health system, the Slovenian government is continuing to issue certificates for private primary care practices. This process is being opposed by an initiative to preserve publicly provided health services on the grounds that the privatization process is uncontrolled and lacks transparency, and that there should have been a public call for tenders.

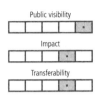

Since 1992, when the privatization of the provision of services in the health system was placed on a legal footing again, it has been a topic of constant public debate. The intensity of the disputes rises and falls, depending on the government in power. With the change of government in 2004, the new government made privatization of the public sector and thus also of the health system one of its top priorities. The aim of the policy is to introduce more flexibility in the system by means of private services in primary care and to make the provision of services more economically efficient and more oriented to the actual needs of the local populations.

Privatization— a topic since 1992

Doctors can establish themselves independently or in a group with other doctors. The incentives are that a doctor working privately in a well-run practice can generate a higher income and can be independent of the public system. So far it has been possible to note a positive development regarding flexibility and patient satisfaction. Surveys and studies show that patients are satisfied with the private services. A survey of members of the Slovenian Medical Council showed that 70 percent to 75 percent of service providers are interested in setting up privately.

More scope for doctors

The privatization process is dogged by two problems. First, one of the main actors in the Slovenian health service, the Association of Public Providers of Health Care, which also represents all

Two main problems of privatization

centers for public primary care, is opposed to the privatization. Second, it is necessary to reorganize the established rights and responsibilities for the provision of services. However, it is unclear whether regulatory responsibilities will be shifted from the local authorities to the regional or national level. The government is required to ensure fair access and free choice for patients and service providers in the health system. However, in the past it has only been able to influence the local authorities to increase the calls for offers from private service providers.

Does the United States show what privatization leads to?

Opponents of privatization advance the following arguments:

- The health ministry is in contravention of EU legislation because the private service providers were not selected on the basis of public procurement rules, but in an administrative process.
- Privatization leads to higher expenditure on health care as a percentage of GDP.
- The introduction of private health insurance—also a topic of public debate in Slovenia—is leading to a differentiation between patients on the basis of their financial potential.
- Since private healthcare providers put profits first, they are not suited to provide the best care for their patients.
- The United States shows what a liberalized, primarily private, system leads to.

Opposition blocks the process

The conflict with the opposition about this topic grew, and as a result privatization came to an almost complete standstill. The opposition has been supported by various trade unions, by managers of institutions providing public services, and by scientists. The opposition, for its part, supports the new Movement to Maintain Public Providers in the Health Service. They see themselves as the defenders of fair access to health care by public providers of services.

Draft law intended to create order

The health ministry has announced a new law for private registration in the health system, which is intended to bring order to the registration process. When the process of drafting the legislation has been completed, it will be presented for public discussion. But the more public the discussion, the more vocally the opponents will register their objections.

Sources and further reading:
Albreht, Tit. "Privatization of health care in Slovenia." *Health Policy Monitor*, August 2005. www.hpm.org/survey/si/a5/1.
Albreht, Tit. "Public debates on privatization." *Health Policy Monitor*, October 2006. www.hpm.org/survey/si/a8/2.

Reform tracker

Austria

Canada

Mental health
National strategy for mental health; VII/VIII, 56

Patients' safety
Institute for patient safety, V; 37

Quality management
Barcelona and Montreal compare their healthcare services; IV, 61
Independent council for quality improvement; I, 37
Independent council for quality improvement in health care; II, 85

Denmark

Access
No-show fees for non-attending patients; IV, 39

Accountability and participation
An open and transparent healthcare system; III, 22

Evaluation in health care
Evaluation of DRG system; VI, 30

Funding and reimbursement
The search for the right mix of roles; I, 31

Health and aging
Free choice of provider of personal and practical help; II, 31

Pharmaceutical policies
Emphasis on economic evaluation of new pharmaceuticals; II, 56

Public health and prevention
More signs instead of less smoke; V, 66

(Re-)centralization versus decentralization
Strategy for the healthcare system—The patient; III, 44
Public sector reform and hospital management—A political
agreement; IV, 79

236

Technical innovations and bioethics
Electronic patient records in hospitals; III, 53
Sobering evaluation of electronic patient records in hospitals; VI, 60

Estonia

Information and communication technologies
National health information system; VI, 62

Need-based care
Family doctor hotline 24/7; VII/VIII, 122

Finland

Access
Supplementary outpatient fees; IV, 36
Better access to dental care for adults; VII/VIII, 75

Accountability and participation
Vouchers in social and health care; III, 24

Funding and reimbursement
Plans to reform the hospital billing system; I, 32

Health reform—from idea to implementation
Government successfully enforces shorter waiting times;
VII/VIII, 42

Pharmaceutical policies
Generic substitution of prescription drugs; II, 59
New Development Center for Drug Therapy; II, 60
Restricting generic substitution; IV, 77
Expensive drugs for rare diseases; V, 76
Reform package for pharmaceuticals; VI, 90

Primary care
Research in primary care centers; V, 86

Public health and prevention
Major reduction in alcohol tax; V, 59
Smoking bans in bars and restaurants; VII/VIII, 216

Quality management
The debate about the right level of specialized care; I, 40
Hospital evaluation for increased cost-effectiveness; VII/VIII, 118

(Re-)centralization versus decentralization
County-level management of welfare services; III, 44

France

Access
Health insurance vouchers plan; IV, 29
Health insurance reform; II, 76
High council on the future of sickness insurance; III, 67
Health insurance credits for the needy—only modest success;
VII/VIII, 105

Funding and reimbursement
Hôpital 2007; V, 27
Ambulatory care system caught between physicians and
private insurance; V, 30

Health and aging
Toward long-term care reform; II, 35

Human resources for health
Observation and monitoring of health professionals; VI, 76
Plan for demographic development of doctors; VII/VIII, 163

Integration of care/coordination of care
Toward a nursing care plan for the disabled; I, 48

Pharmaceutical policies
Lower reimbursement rates and delisting of pharmaceuticals; II, 50
Liberalization of prices for innovative medicines; II, 52

Primary care
Improved coordination in health care; IV, 47

Public health and prevention
Draft five-year public health plan; I, 53
Reform of the public health law; III, 40
Ambitious public health policy threatened, V, 45

Quality management
Quality benchmarks to reduce infections in hospitals;
VII/VIII, 115

Technical innovations and bioethics
Bioethics legislation; III, 55

Germany

Funding and reimbursement
Co-payments for ambulatory care, V; 22

Health and aging
Proposals to achieve financial sustainability of LTCI; II, 40

Human resources for health
Improving healthcare structures with nurse practitioners;
VII/VIII, 151

Integration of care/coordination of care
Disease management programs combine quality and financial
incentives; III, 32
Integrated care contracts; VI, 45

Primary care
Family doctors as gatekeepers; IV, 52

Quality management
Plans for a "Center for Quality in Medicine"; I, 38
Compulsory external quality assurance for hospitals; IV, 56

Israel

Access
Co-payments, access, equity; IV, 30
Information brochure on long-term care comes with
the newspaper; VII/VIII, 124

Advancing healthcare organization
For-profit sickness fund; IV, 65

Evaluation in health care
Audit for hospital licensing; VI, 26

Health and aging
Keeping the elderly fit and healthy; VII/VIII, 141

Human resources for health
Community training for specialists; VI, 80

Information and communication technologies
Institutions sharing electronic medical records; VI, 58

Need-based care
Treatment of mental illness in primary care; VII/VIII, 59
E-learning program in women's health; VII/VIII, 63

Primary care
Improvement of primary care quality; IV, 51

Public health and prevention
Health plans assume responsibility for preventive care; V, 47
Sharon's illness raises interest in stroke prevention; VII/VIII, 207

Health and aging
End-of-life care policy; V, 82

Japan

Netherlands

Health reform – from idea to implementation
Healthcare reform 2006—Good things come to those who wait,
or intentional salami tactics?; VII/VIII, 25

Human resources for health
Coping with prospective shortages in the medical work force;
II, 70

Quality management
Compulsory quality improvement; I, 42
Quality management more compulsory; II, 84

New Zealand

Access
Lower co-payments for visits to general practitioners;
VII/VIII, 78

Evaluation in health care
Performance Evaluation Programme; VI, 27

Funding and reimbursement
Prepaid general practice fee; I, 22

Health and aging
Removal of assets test for older people in long-term residential care;
II, 42
Aging in place—projects and evaluation; VII/VIII, 137

Human resources for health
Workforce development; II, 72
Further development of nursing care; VII/VIII, 154

Information and communication technologies
Electronic support for clinical decisions; VI, 68

Mental health
A national mental health plan; IV, 23

Pharmaceutical policies
Direct-to-consumer advertising of prescription medicines; II, 66
Continued unlimited advertisement of medicines?; VII/VIII, 191

Public health and prevention
Cancer control action plan, V, 49
100 percent smoke-free, V, 64
Let's beat Diabetes; VII/VIII, 200
Suicide prevention strategy 2006–2016; VII/VIII, 202

Primary care
Care Plus for high-needs patients; IV, 45
Primary health organizations; I, 55

Quality management
Improving quality—A strategic approach; II, 87

(Re-)centralization versus decentralization
Interim evaluation of district health boards; III, 50

Poland

Evaluation in health care
Agency for Health Technology Assessment; VI, 24

Pharmaceutical policy
More transparency in drug reimbursements; VII/VIII, 185

Singapore

Access
Reform of Medishield high-risk insurance; VII/VIII, 80

Funding and reimbursement
ElderShield—Supplementary insurance for long-term care; I, 26
Medisave and MediShield withdrawal limits; I, 27
Increase in Medisave withdrawal limits; II, 81

Portability of employment medical benefits; II, 82
HealthConnect—A community health care model; IV, 72
New financing for outpatient disease management programs;
VII/VIII, 109

Health and aging
Integration of acute medical care, inpatient recovery and
rehabilitation care; VII/VIII, 135

Human resources for health
Upgrading family medicine; VI, 85

Information and communication technologies
Web transparency reduces hospital bills, V, 85
Outsourcing x-ray analysis to India; VII/VIII, 171

Need-based care
Outpatient DMPs for the chronically ill; VII/VIII, 66

Technical innovations and bioethics
Amendments to the Human Organ Transplant Act; III, 57

Slovenia

Funding and reimbursement
Risk-structure compensation for supplementary insurance;
VII/VIII, 107

Human resources for health
Independent specialists; VI, 81
Struggle with a shortage of nurses; VII/VIII, 168

Primary care
Public debate about the privatization of primary care; VII/VIII, 229

South Korea

Advancing healthcare organization
Merger of health insurance societies in 2000; II, 77

Pharmaceutical policies
Separation of drug prescribing and dispensing; II, 64

Public health and prevention
Tobacco tax increase proposal; III, 38
Tobacco tax and health promotion; V, 63
Health promotion with traditional medicine; VII/VIII, 197

Reimbursement
Extending the benefit basket; VI, 89

Quality management
Evaluation of hospitals; IV, 62

Spain

Access
Facilitating specialized services and medication for
illegal immigrants; IV, 33

Funding and reimbursement
National insurance for long-term care; VII/VIII, 102

Health and aging
Second plan for integrating health and social care in Castile and
Leon; II, 28
Toledo Agreement and LTC insurance; II, 33

Information and communication technologies
Spain and the United States: electronic prescriptions;
VII/VIII, 187

Integration of care/coordination of care
A pilot project for integrated care in Catalonia; I, 50
The Denia Model; VI, 48

Pharmaceutical policies
Reference pricing system for generic medicines: Update and extension; II, 62
Pharmaceutical reform in decentralized healthcare system; V, 78
Draft legislation to rationalize use of pharmaceuticals; VII/VIII, 182

Public health and prevention
Weak anti-tobacco law, V, 61

Quality management
Barcelona and Montreal compare their healthcare services; IV, 61
National Health System Act—The debate about decentralization, cohesion and quality of care; I, 43

(Re-)centralization versus decentralization
Evaluating regional healthcare financing; III, 49

Technical innovations and bioethics
Electronic drug management; III, 54

Switzerland

Advancing healthcare organization
Relaunching integrated networks of care; IV, 70

Emerging issues
Health-impact assessment of Ticino's public policy; IV, 24

Evaluation in health care
The evaluation program of complementary medicine; VI, 21

England: NHS foundation trusts; I, 34
Practice-based commissioning for GPs; VII/VIII, 51
New funding system for dental treatment; VII/VIII, 169

Health and aging
England: National Service Framework for older people; II, 30
United Kingdom: Recent reforms of policy on long-term care for elderly people; II, 43

Health reforms – from idea to implementation
Ten years of Labour – more market, more choice in healthcare; VII/VIII, 38

Human resources for health
General practitioners and health trainers for disadvantaged areas; VI, 83

Integration of care/coordination of care
England: The management of chronic diseases; III, 31
England and Wales: Reforms in social care; VI, 41

Pharmaceutical policies
England and Wales: Health technology assessment and the National Institute for Clinical Excellence; II, 54

Primary care
United Kingdom: The new general practitioner contract; IV, 44
Public contributes to primary care decisions; VII/VIII, 120

Public health and prevention
England: Wanless Reports—Health spending and public health; III, 39
England: National screening program for bowel cancer, V, 51

Quality management
England: NHS Foundation Trusts; IV, 59

United States

Notes

Notes

Notes

Notes

Notes

Notes